BUILD YOUR
BRAIN POWER

BUILD YOUR BRAIN POWER

*The Latest Techniques
to Preserve, Restore,
and Improve Your
Brain's Potential*

Arthur Winter, M.D., and Ruth Winter

ST. MARTIN'S • NEW YORK

Design by Victoria Hartman

Library of Congress Cataloging in Publication Data

Winter, Arthur, 1922–
    Build your brain power.

    1. Intellect—Problems, exercises, etc. I. Winter,
Ruth, 1930–   . II. Title.
BF431.3.W56 1986   153   85-26156
ISBN 0-312-10768-4

First Edition

10 9 8 7 6 5 4 3 2 1

To Rosie, Robin, Craig, Grant, and Jonathan.
Love stimulates the brain.

Contents

Acknowledgments

The authors wish to thank the many who gave of their time and knowledge now and in the past, particularly: Floyd Bloom, M.D., director of the Pre-Clinical Neurosciences and Endocrinology, The Scripps Clinic and Research Foundation; Ranjan Duara, M.D., formerly of The National Institutes of Health; Irene Parese, Ph.D, director of The Cognitive Remediation Program, The Kessler Institute, East Orange, New Jersey; Irwin Pollock, M.D., director of The Rutgers Medical School Cognitive Rehabilitation Program, New Brunswick, New Jersey; Yehuda Ben-Yishay, Ph.D., co-director of the Head Trauma Program, New York University Medical Center; Alma Christine Connor, Sylvia Barrasso, and Louise Noll, librarians, St. Barnabas Medical Center, Livingston, New Jersey; and Lynn Maxwell, special education teacher, Plainview, New York.

Introduction

To the neurosurgeon, the brain is the greatest machine on earth. He may study and repair it when possible, but he never loses the wonder at the genius of its creation.

To the science writer, the brain is a subject that is always intriguing, with new discoveries constantly being made and many mysteries yet to be solved.

Together, we have studied and interviewed and searched to produce this book. The field of neuroscience is the fastest-growing scientific discipline, and the thousands of researchers who are working in it are producing mountains of information. It is frustrating and fascinating that though we may all receive an identical stimulation, our brains will interpret it differently. There are controversies and false leads about neurophysiology, but it is incontestable that great progress is being made in understanding how the brain functions. One of the most fruitful areas of research and the one upon which we have based this book concerns brain potential. It is now clear that your brain can be developed and repaired to a degree, even in old age. The "degree" often depends on the one thing that no one yet understands clearly—motivation.

You are using only a fraction of your true brain potential.

We have described the latest research and techniques

available to increase your brain power. In this book, we hope to stimulate you and help you develop and maintain your brain to near its maximum capacity.

We can present the facts, theories, and techniques, but it is up to you to make the effort.

Arthur Winter, M.D.,
and Ruth Winter, B.A., Livingston, N.J.

1

The Plastic Brain and How It Grows

Just as you can train your body to increase in strength and fitness, so you can train your brain to preserve, restore, and improve your intellect through selective stimulation.

Your brain is better designed than any machine on earth and far superior to the brains used by other living creatures. It has the capacity to gather and store an infinite amount of information from without and within and to manipulate that data instantly, not only as it has done in the past but in new ways. It is constantly trying to understand itself.

You use only a fraction of your brain's capacity—an estimated .01 percent to 10 percent. And, like many other people, you may abuse your brain by hitting it, bathing it in noxious chemicals, depriving it of necessary nutrients, and allowing it to go "flabby," like a potbelly.

A tremendous revolution has taken place in how science interprets brains and cognition. Until recently, it was believed that as the years passed, the normal human brain inevitably declined in function and that there was nothing much that could be done about it. New information has been gathered by a wide variety of experts, including neuroscientists and gerontologists who have been able to listen to a single brain cell "talking." Studies of thousands of people and of anatomic specimens over a long period of time have found that decline is by no means inevitable,[1-7] and that there is very little difference in functional capacity between the brains of healthy young people and those of healthy older people.

Ranjan Duara, M.D., formerly of the National Institutes of Health, and his colleagues at NIH used one of the newer techniques, the PET scan (Positron Emission Tomography), to study the difference between the metabolism of younger and older brains. (Metabolism refers to the brain's use of its fuel, such as the sugar glucose, to function.) During the sessions, volunteers between the ages of 20 and 80 were injected with radioactive glucose. Their ears were plugged and their eyes masked, but they were instructed not to fall asleep, just to relax. Forty-five minutes later, after the radioactive material had been absorbed, the subjects placed their heads in a holder that fits inside a metal cylinder.[8]

The volunteers were given a series of geometric designs to copy at their leisure and a few other noncompetitive tasks. As they performed these assignments with their heads in the cylinder, doctors monitored where the radioactive-tagged glucose went, pinpointing the area of the brain being used to "perform" or to "think" about the task.

"There was no significant difference in metabolism between the healthy older brains and the healthy younger ones in a resting state," Duara said. "There were some variations noted more commonly in older subjects, but they were not universal. Some men in their eighties had exactly the same brain metabolism as much younger men, while some younger men showed the changes usually observed in older brains."

There are common age changes in the brain, of course, just as there are wrinkles on the skin. CAT scans (computerized X-rays) do show that there is a degree of atrophy, and the brains of most 70-year-olds are lighter in weight than those of average 20-year-olds. The joints and muscles of a 45-year-old are not, on the average, as flexible as those of a 25-year-old. The difference that really counts is how the brain and body function. A trained and motivated 37-year-old Carlos Lopes of Portugal could beat men in their early twenties in the 1984 Olympic marathon. Older people of the same basic intelligence as 20-year-olds may perform better mentally because the seniors have continued to train their brains.

But like wrinkles, not everyone gets the age changes in the brain at the same time, and not everyone gets as many as everyone else. In some people, such alterations are virtually imperceptible.

This point was made clear when Congress asked the National Institutes of Health and the Secretary of Transportation in 1979 to study the "Age 60 rule," which forced commercial pilots to retire. After ten months, the study committee concluded that "variability [in the effects of aging] within an age group is often nearly as great as variability between different age groups, and that usually no single age emerges as a point of sharp decline. . . . Available evidence suggests that on the average at least some of the skills necessary to the highest level of safety deteriorate with age. However, there is great variation among individuals within any age group. . . ."[9]

The long-accepted belief that we all lose a great many brain cells as we age was based on faulty research. Marian Cleeves Diamond, Ph.D., professor of anatomy at the University of California at Irvine, explained why: "They took the brain of a healthy 8-year-old and compared it to the brain of a sick 80-year-old and found there was a decrease in the surface area of from 10 to 20 percent, and that was interpolated that we all lose 100,000 brain cells after the age of 30. People accepted this. But the brains they studied were inactive, degenerate brains, and naturally you are going to see a loss of cells. If you look at healthy brains, you don't find this loss."[10]

In fact, working with mice in the laboratory, Dr. Diamond and her colleagues discovered that an enriched environment could increase the weight of the brain, even in older animals. Dr. Diamond, practicing what she has observed, takes singing lessons to enrich her brain and her life.[11]

Challenging your brain to keep it in optimal condition is vital not only to your central nervous system but to your entire body.

Your brain is the most important part of your nervous system—the captain of its organization. For your body to survive, your nervous system must be maintained. All your other organs will undergo sacrifice to keep your brain going when you are under severe stress. The brain's mastery over even a failing body can be very dramatic. What viewer was not moved by the almost unconscious Gabriella Andersen-Scheisse struggling to get over the finish line of the 1984 Olympic marathon despite the almost complete exhaustion of her body?

The brain, by weight alone, is 90 percent of the central nervous system. There is also a long extension of the brain descending inside the neck and backbone, known as the spinal cord. From both the brain and the spinal cord, nerves go out to the sensory organs: the eyes, ears, and nose. Nerves also go out to muscles, to skin, and to all the other organs of the body.

One of the major functions of the central nervous system is communication—communication within its various parts and with the outside world. The signals that communicate information within the brain are electrical and chemical in nature: Within individual nerve cells, or neurons, the signals are predominantly electrical; the signals that are transmitted from one neuron to another, conversely, are largely chemical.

As new discoveries about the human brain are made within a wide variety of disciplines, old beliefs and research conclusions are being proved wrong. Until quite recently, for example, communication between the nerves was thought to occur only at specialized junctions between cells called *synapses*. It has now been discovered that nerves not only produce chemicals that affect adjoining nerves but can issue substances that travel throughout the body, affecting other nerves at distant sites. It was also believed that only one chemical was active at one synapse. Now it has been observed that several chemicals may be sent out and received at a single site. Furthermore, it was assumed that the axon, the long "wire" that carries the nerve signal, was only a one-way channel. Recently, it has been reported that the flow of signals, just like a telephone conversation, goes in two directions.[12-14] And, it was once thought that dendrites, those spiderlike endings that arise from the main nerve root, were only receivers of signals. Now it appears that they may leak substances in the opposite direction.[15]

The explosion of knowledge in neurobiology has just begun. New information about the human brain is growing so rapidly that it really does boggle the mind. And one of the most important and intriguing findings is that damage to the central nervous system is not necessarily irreparable, as previously maintained, and that critical mental and motor functions may be restored either by nerves forming new connections or shunting signals around injured-tissue roadblocks. Furthermore, decline in mental function is not an inevitable part of aging.

The brain is composed of two types of cells, glia and neurons. Glia, named for the Greek word meaning "glue," were once thought to be merely supporting cells but have now been found to take care of many of the basic biochemical chores, including producing nerve coverings that aid in transmission and neurochemical production.

Neurons, on the other hand, perform the main work of the brain, processing impulses from far-flung nerves of the sense organs. Much of this activity is concentrated in the cortex, the thick, folded outer layer of the brain. Groups of neurons on the surface of the cortex process the complex stream of information flowing constantly from the eyes, ears, and other sense organs and nerves throughout the body. The neurons convey these electrical and chemical messages to deeper layers of the cortex and to other underlying brain structures as well as outward to muscles and organs.

Dr. Diamond and her group, as well as others, have shown that the glial cells of mice brains, which provide support and aid to the neurons, remain in number, even in old age, and are capable of being increased merely by an enrichment of their environment, even in very elderly mice.[16] The same is undoubtedly true of humans. In fact, Dr. Diamond found when examining a specimen from the brain of the genius Albert Einstein that his brain had 73 percent more glial cells than the average for humans.

A MOTOR NERVE

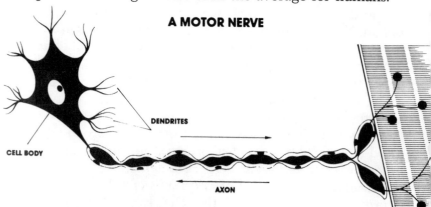

DENDRITES

CELL BODY

AXON

In long-term studies of humans, it has also been shown that people who continue to be active intellectually can actually improve on intelligence tests beyond the age of 60 years.[17-18]

Our brains have been designed so well that despite some damage or neglect, we have enough spare capacity that we can often overcome intellectual malfunctions. In fact, the new science of cognitive rehabilitation now being developed to help those whose brains have been severely injured by accidents or strokes has already proven the amazing ability of the brain to overcome deficits by retraining. For example:

• In a severe and often fatal type of stroke called the "Locked-In Syndrome," all four limbs and the speech center of the brain are paralyzed. Some patients, however, eventually recover enough brain function to return to their homes, walk again, and lead fairly normal lives.[19]

• An American tank commander under attack in Vietnam was firing his machine gun when there was a blast next to him. It wasn't until he ran out of ammunition and had to reach down with his left hand to get a new belt that he realized he couldn't use his left hand and that there

THE BRAIN

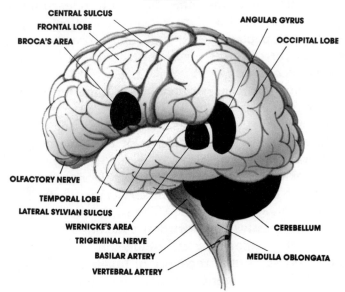

CENTRAL SULCUS
FRONTAL LOBE
BROCA'S AREA
ANGULAR GYRUS
OCCIPITAL LOBE
OLFACTORY NERVE
TEMPORAL LOBE
LATERAL SYLVIAN SULCUS
WERNICKE'S AREA
TRIGEMINAL NERVE
BASILAR ARTERY
VERTEBRAL ARTERY
CEREBELLUM
MEDULLA OBLONGATA

was something wrong. He was missing a quarter of his brain.[20]

• A 65-year-old college professor suffered a massive stroke that left him with little muscle control in the right side of his body. Though few specialists thought he would regain his functions, the man recovered fully after five years of active home therapy. Years later, after the professor died of a heart attack while mountain climbing, autopsy revealed the extent of damage caused by the stroke. A large area of the left side of the brain and the pyramidal tract—the region controlling many voluntary muscle movements—had been destroyed. Some other part of the brain had assumed the functions that the damaged area had once controlled."[21]

• A 44-year-old professor of psychology had a cardiac arrest in which the oxygen was cut off and the right side of his brain was damaged. He awoke in the hospital unable to recall how many children he had. He thought he was ten years younger than he was and he couldn't remember the way to his home. He had to relearn how to play the stereo, set the alarm clock, use a calculator, and change a razor blade.[22-23] It took him more than seven years, but through a great deal of hard and innovative work, he recovered from his deficits and today is teaching full-time and is in charge of clinical training for graduate psychology students at his former university.

Obviously, recovery from severe brain damage is possible. Intelligence evidently has a lot to do with it. The Vietnam Head Injury Study at Walter Reed Army Medical Center compared post-injury intelligence data with intelligence data obtained from servicemen before they were severely brain injured.[24] The researchers who conducted the massive investigation concluded that a person's "level of experience or intelligence" before a head injury is critical to the recovery of function. The higher the patient's intelligence score before injury, the less likely he is "to show loss" on a post-injury intelligence test. The intelligence factor, they found, is even more important than the size or location of the brain lesion.

It is significant that in the study of Vietnam veterans and many other studies, a capacity that is vital but that neuroscientists and psychologists have not been able to measure is *motivation*. This mysterious factor can help one patient with severe brain damage make greater progress than another with much less damage.[25-27] It also applies to healthy people and is a positive factor in everyday living.

Those who have suffered brain damage within the past few years, such as the psychology professor mentioned above, are benefiting from those practicing in the new field of cognitive rehabilitation. Cognitive psychology has borrowed from the techniques developed by experts treating children with learning problems. So, too, we have borrowed techniques from cognitive rehabilitation and the learning disabled that can be adapted to enable healthy people "brain build," just as those in pursuit of physical fitness "body build." Brain fitness involves motivation, repetition, and "stretching" to improve cognition.

Cognition, by definition, means the process of perceiving or knowing. It includes the following:

• Focusing and sustaining attention.
• Differentiating between what is relevant and what is not.
• Memorizing—encoding and storing information.
• Organizing and integrating.
• Problem solving.
• Transmitting and communicating.
• Creating new ways to process and use data.

You cannot change your heredity or your age, just as you cannot change your basic bone structure, but you can develop the brain you were given to a much greater capacity. Your brain, just like your muscles, will atrophy if not continually used.

It has been determined that your brain and peripheral nervous system are like telephone wires that carry conversations back and forth. Specific stimulation will keep your "wires" flowing with the information that initiates the internal and external signals for your thoughts and actions.

It is not too late to start "brain building." Your brain and your nerves are capable of repair and growth in adulthood. In the World Health Organization's *Treatise on Neuroplasticity and Repair in the Central Nervous System* (Geneva, Switzerland, 1983), the general principles state:

> Neuroplasticity does not concern only the recovery of function if this latter is defined as "a return to normal or near-normal levels of performance," following the initially disruptive effects of injury to the nervous system. Neuroplasticity does not refer only to the structural and functional changes of the neuronal organization which follow an injury, but also includes the capacity of the central nervous system to adapt to new physiological conditions emerging either during its maturation or its interaction with the environment. Therefore, neuroplasticity consists of the ability of the nervous system to adapt (in both an anatomical and a functional sense) its structural organization to new situations emerging from developmental and environmental influences as well as from injuries.

In this book, you will read descriptions of exercises for various cognitive functions and some of the theory behind their use. You will learn to use your brain to exercise itself and "stretch" its own capacity.

2

How to Be Sensational—
Perfecting Your Perceptions

Your brain and nerves have a basic function: to assist you in adapting to perceived changes inside and outside your body. Your "nervous system" accomplishes this by processing information from your senses.

For example, take an apple in your hand.

Now, how do you know that what you have in your hand is an apple?

First of all, when you took it in your hand, you excited numerous minute sense organs scattered in and below your skin, some of which were particularly sensitive to touch, others to pressure, and still others to temperature.

The little sense organs sent the fact that you were feeling something cold, round, and smooth to your spinal cord, which in turn relayed the message to your brain.

At the same time, light rays reflected from the surface of the apple stimulated the nerve cells in your eyes. The nerve cells immediately reported back to your brain that you had a red, shiny, round object in your hand.

Still simultaneously, minuscule particles bounding from the apple to the surrounding air excited the tiny nerve cells inside your nose and told your brain how the object in your hand smelled.

Your brain computed all the information you sent it in a time almost too short to calculate, and because it had long ago recorded the fact that a cold, smooth, shiny, round, red, sweet-smelling object is an apple, you realized you had an apple in your hand.

If your brain were to tell you not to eat the apple because it had a worm in it, that would be another story.

This brings us to how you gather information for processing by your brain and how you can maintain and even sharpen your ability to do so.

Any physical change that affects your senses—touch, hearing, sight, smell, and taste—affects your degree of consciousness.

There are your interior senses—hunger, thirst, fatigue, and pain perception. Another sense, that of equilibrium, or balance, tells you of your position in space, right side up or upside down. Still another sense, proprioception, tells you of your activity with the aid of tiny receptors inside your muscles and joints. Most of us aren't even aware that we have proprioception, yet we use this muscular sense to determine where in space something is that we are touching and whether it is heavy, light, soft, hard, or gaseous. Here is a simple experiment that illustrates this marvelous, often unheralded sense.

Test Your Proprioception Perception
Take several different-sized cans from your pantry shelf. Place them on the kitchen counter. Now, close your eyes and lift each one up, and by feel alone place them in descending order of weight. Open your eyes and check your evaluation. How did you know which ones were heavier and which ones were lighter? You used your proprioception sense.

Nerve endings sensitive to movement or pressure are buried in strategic places inside your body. They feed your brain, via your spinal cord, information vital for working your muscles, and they automatically adjust your limbs and body. They also are involved in the control of your internal organs. Such proprioceptors occur in skeletal and respiratory muscles and are stimulated when the muscle is stretched or shortened. Inside the receptors, which are wound around the striations of the muscles, are specialized fibers containing fine motor nerves; these nerves are believed to be controlled by the cerebellum. Muscles that perform complex, delicate maneuvers, such as those in the fingers and feet, have more spindles per gram of muscle than those that perform less complex movements, such as calf muscles.

HOW DISTANT ARE YOU?

We also have a mysterious sense of distance or space. In fact, the problem of what process an animal uses to locate itself in space is one that has puzzled researchers for a long time. How are animals able to follow novel routes to goals? A concept gaining greater acceptance today is that an animal has a brain map for each environment with which it is familiar; the "map" may be in the lower center of the brain in an area shaped like a seahorse and given the Greek name for that creature, the hippocampus. The "seahorse" is involved in recent memory and behavior. Researchers have discovered that most nerves in the hippocampus fire "spatially."[1] That is, an individual nerve cell "lights up" only when a rat, for example, is in one portion of its environment. Just like light bulbs on a marquee, each cell has its own active region—its spatial field. When they are "turned on" in a certain pattern, they spell out a star's name on a marquee or a location on a brain map. This suggests that the hippocampus is part of a nerve network that informs the rat just where it is in a particular environment.

Since a rat can find its way around many different environments, researchers now theorize that hippocampal cells can discriminate between shapes like rectangles and cylinders and thus are sensitive to the global features of an environment. They can reflect the panoramic picture as well as being "turned on" by a particular shape within the picture.

These findings support the idea that rats do indeed have an environmental space map and that the hippocampal cells are sensitive to the geometry of the enclosure in which the rat is placed.[2]

Do we humans have similar nerve maps in our brains? It is now believed that our hippocampus may help answer two of our own spatial questions: "What sort of environment am I in?" and "Where am I in this environment?"

Fingering Space

Shut your eyes and place your hands at your sides. Now, slowly bring just the tips of your two index fingers together in front of you. Do this four times. How did you know where to touch?

We don't usually exercise our sense of space, because we rely so heavily on our eyes to tell us where we are, but we all have it. As we walk down a dark hallway, for example, we become aware, without touching the wall, that the hallway ends. This may be due to changes in reflected sounds, air pressure, or scent from the walls. The sense of space can be well developed, particularly in blind people.

Finding Your Way With Your Eyes Closed

Choose a blank wall or a closed door. Stand about five feet back. Close your eyes and inch your way very slowly toward the wall or door until you believe you are an inch from it. Open your eyes. How accurate were you?

You can sharpen your sense of space by periodically closing your eyes and, without touching walls or furniture, finding your way along a familiar path, such as the route from your bedroom to your bathroom. Clear away all objects in your path first and, of course, go slowly. Don't try it if you have trouble with your balance.

WHAT TIME IS IT?

Still another wonderful sense we use but often do not realize we have is our sense of time.

Short periods of time are difficult to assess unless you count your pulse or notice environmental changes. Longer periods of time can be estimated by observing light changes and hunger sensations and other body functions such as the desire to eliminate wastes. Still, your sense of time is quite accurate. Test yourself: Look at your watch and observe the time. Now, close your eyes. Don't count. Just sit quietly and when you believe three minutes have passed, look at your watch again and check to see how close you were. Do this whenever you are standing in line or waiting in an office for an appointment. It will not only pass the time, it will help sharpen your sense of time.

It is accepted today from studies of the nervous system and behavior that sensory input is critically important for normal development. And yet none of us fully develops our senses, just as we never use all our brain power, unless circumstances require it.

Helen Keller, for example, who was blind and deaf, could tell a storm's approach before anyone else. She smelled it.

While most of us do not have to concentrate on one sense as Helen Keller did for information processing, we usually favor one sense over another.

A wine connoisseur, for example, can often tell the vineyard in which a wine was grown and even the year. He or she has developed senses of taste and smell. A perfumer can walk into your home and identify your cleaning compounds and what you had for dinner the past two nights just by sniffing the air.

An art critic, on the other hand, may look at a few dots of color on a canvas and declare it art worthy of a museum, or a marksman may hit a small, moving target at a great distance by looking through a scope. They've both concentrated on their sense of sight.

Do you love music? It may be the sense organs on the side of your head—your ears—that you favor.

Do you like the feel of velvet? Are you a "toucher"?

Our senses are not only vital for information processing and self-protection, they are the means by which we enjoy living.

One of the fascinating characteristics about perception and sensual pleasure is that they are very brief. Stimulation does not persist with equal response over a period of time. The stimulus must be varied with intervals of rest to remain effective. A popular tune that at first you can't hear often enough will, after prolonged playing, become boring. Eating the same meal, no matter how tasty, will become unappetizing and, thus, most people vary their menus.

Fatigue Your Senses

Press your arm against the wall as hard as you can for the count of 30. Then walk away. Your arm will feel lighter than usual. You have fatigued the nerve cells in your arm and affected how your brain senses it.

Copy the spiral on the next page, punch a hole in the center and spin it on your record player or on a pencil, and stare at it for one minute. Then look at a blank wall or door. What do you see? The spiral will usually go in the opposite direction. This effect is believed to be caused by the tiring of the nerve cells registering movement in the first direction and the "overflow" firing of the nerve cells detecting movements in the opposite direction.

Every sensory experience is appreciated within the context of previous experiences. A child may prefer the most intense, novel sensory experiences, but when the novelty wears off, he becomes bored with them. This search for strong sensation is one of the major reasons some people seek the "thrill" of psychoactive drugs or unusual sexual exploits. But such a quest is usually endless because the more intense a sensation, the quicker it is gone. On the other hand, if we learn to modulate our senses and develop them even in advanced years, we increase our pleasure in living and we maintain normal function in the cells that receive and respond to sensual input. A decrease in sensory input due to changes in the sense organs or to social isolation is reflected in reduced metabolism and blood flow within the brain.[3] The following information is about the research in progress to understand the interrelationship between our brains and our sense organs. Selective stimulation through conscious effort will enable you to keep the messages flowing that provide you with information about the world around you and the pleasures that give your life meaning.

THE EYES HAVE IT

The sense organs of sight, hearing, touch, taste, and smell report to and are perceived in the cerebral cortex, a huge sheet covering the surface of your brain. It contains as many as ten thousand million nerve cells—neurons—and the "sheet" is folded to fit inside the skull, giving the "brain" that many-convoluted look. It has been found that a light held above the head evokes nerve-cell activity in a different part of the cortex than does a light held below the head. Similarly a light held directly in front of the viewer activates different parts of the brain's cortex than a light held off to the side. Nerve cells of the visual cortex, the part of the brain to which the eyes report, are highly specialized information-processing machines. It is again similar to light bulbs on a theater marquee. Just as the hippocampal cells "light up" in a certain pattern in response to the environment, the cells of the visual cortex respond to what is seen in a highly specialized manner. Only certain things turn individual cells on.

The Nobel Prize–winning studies of David Hubel and Torsten Wiesel first showed that nerve cells in the cortical area of the brain can only be activated by specific features of what the eyes see.[4] Cortical nerve cells are very often excited more strongly by inputs from one eye than the other. Hubel and Wiesel showed that nerve cells that preferred one eye were *clustered* within the cortex, and segregated from nerve cells preferring the other eye. Furthermore, some of the nerve cells that "see" in the brain prefer vertical bars, others horizontal, and still others are partial to the oblique. Again, nerve cells that respond to one kind of shape are clustered together within the brain.

Flashlight Exercises

The purpose of the following "flashlight" exercises is to stimulate the various areas of your brain involved in light perception.

Take a flashlight, preferably a penlight. Hold it over your head while looking straight ahead, and then look up at the light without moving your head. Lower the flashlight to below your chin, again without moving your head, and look down at the light. Count to five and look straight ahead again. Move the flashlight to the right side of your head, about five inches from your ear. Again, without moving your head, look to the light, count to five, then look straight ahead. Repeat the same steps but switch hands, moving the light to the left side of your head.

Take the flashlight and, keeping your head motionless, track the flashlight only with your eyes. Move it very slowly in an arc above your head and down below your chin, then from below your chin to the arc above your head. Repeat five times. Switch hands and repeat.

Now, holding the flashlight, extend your arm out to the side, straight from the shoulder. Pass the flashlight slowly in front of your face at nose level, extending your arm out past the opposite shoulder as far as it will go. Then bring the light slowly back until your arm is at the starting position. Again, track the light only with your eyes. Repeat five times. Put the light in the opposite hand and repeat five times.

Repeat each flashlight exercise with one eye closed. Then repeat with the other eye closed.

Do these exercises at least three times a week.

Ball and String Exercise

Since research now indicates that the perception of moving objects is most seriously affected by age, stimulating the visual sense is important to driving, flying, or occupations that involve working with moving parts. The following exercise[5] is aimed at this:

Hang a ball (or an empty spool of thread) on a string from above five feet high—it can be from a curtain rod or a chandelier or a branch. Swing the ball as hard as you can, sit down, and track its movement with your eyes without moving your head or body. Do this for two minutes. Then move your chair to another position, either sideways or on the opposite side of the hanging ball, and repeat, but again, not for more than two minutes. This helps visual tracking and so does watching a tennis match from the side lines.

Visual Scanning

Visual scanning is necessary for many activities, such as accurately perceiving and locating objects in space, operating a car, and working machinery. Crossword and jigsaw puzzles are excellent for scanning. The following is an exercise to demonstrate your ability to scan.

Find and cross out the letter *S* wherever you find it within 30 seconds.

```
X E D C F S G H J S E T Y X S D Q P O L L G M N B T H H M A S X C V

S E W Q C B G S T N S P O L R T Y U N B F E R W S T Y U J H G B V C

W X C Q A T Y U S D C V H S K L P O B N I Y T H G S F V C B Z A R T

X E R T Y V B D S F E X L K S R U O N M E R S D Q T C V B Y Q P L K

P Z W E Q S C G T S B T B H U I O P L J S D C B T Y H F G K J L S M

O W S Q T Y U K J H G S C V B N M T H S J L W S L F V B T H S N M W

C B V N M J H S D F G H T Y S V C X S B R T C D S T U Y T N M K R S

B D F T R S D U I K L U Y T R P B S C V T E W X Z A Q W S B K I T Y
```

When you are waiting in a doctor's office or a beauty or barber shop, you can take a pencil and cross out a single letter on a printed page. It's a good exercise, if the owner doesn't mind.

Visual-Spatial Orientation
This is a skill needed for identifying and perceiving objects with different forms in various positions.

Circle the objects that are alike in this illustration.

Can You Believe Your Eyes?
When you look at the picture at right, what do you see? An apple tree or a mother and child? Your brain perceives only one image at a time, so your perception may shift back and forth. You may also see something in a picture that another does not see. The famed ink blot or Rorschach test is an example, in which psychotherapists interpret what a person perceives in an irregular stain.

Ignore the "Noise"
Being able to perceive despite background "noise" is an ability that can be improved. For example, look at the following geometric forms and find the designated one in each.

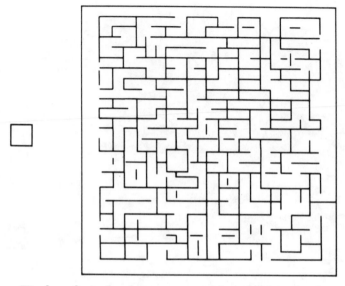

Find and circle the square within four seconds.

Find and circle the circle within three seconds.

LET THERE BE LIGHT

Metabolism refers to the chemical processes through which your body changes air, food, and other materials into substances it needs in order to function properly. The rate at which your metabolism functions may be different from those of other people. It is determined by the genes you inherit and other factors, such as what you eat and the time of day. How you expose yourself to light can also greatly affect your metabolism and your mood and behavior. Light involves intensity, spectrum, and timing.

It has recently been acknowledged that humans, like other animals, can have their hormones manipulated by changing light. The pineal gland in the brain, for example, normally releases its hormone, melatonin, at night and shuts down during the day.

In 1980, Dr. Alfred Lewy, a research psychiatrist then at the National Institute of Mental Health, showed that the release of human melatonin can be blocked by light at least ten times brighter than ordinary room light.[6] He showed that exposure to very bright lights in the visible spectrum during the normally "dark" parts of a person's day could suppress the release of melatonin. He also demonstrated the ability of very bright light in the morning and evening to bring dramatic relief to patients who suffer severe winter-long depressions. You can use light to raise your spirits and to improve your visual perceptions.

• Use a 250-watt bulb in your reading lamps. But the best reading light is still window light. It is brighter and more diffuse, equal to about 5,000 candles.

• Sit closer to the light, within two feet.

• Fluorescent light is very good. It is diffuse and it is cooler and doesn't create a glare.

• When weather permits, open your window. Ordinary

window glass filters out ultraviolet rays. In the winter, spend more time outdoors in the middle of the day, when the light is brightest. Walk to your lunch appointment.

THE SENSE OF HEARING— HAVE YOU HEARD ABOUT IT?

Remember that old nursery rhyme:

> *Here was an old owl liv'd in an oak*
> *The more he heard, the less he spoke*
> *The less he spoke, the more he heard*
> *O, if men were like that wise bird.*

Next to vision, hearing is probably the sense most used to gather information, although some people do have difficulty really listening because they're always talking.

The physiology of the sense of hearing is quite easily measured, since the brain and body are so responsive to sounds. Pleasant auditory stimulation—music, for example—can produce both emotional and physical benefits. One of the reasons that music affects us physically is that it has rhythm (called *pulse*) and tempo *(pace)*, and so do we. The continuous beat of the human heart is the most fundamental of all music rhythms; listen to a primitive drumbeat, for example, and you'll hear a beating heart. Listen to disco music and you'll hear it again. The pulsing beat so closely matches our own heart rate that we feel an urge to move our body in sync with the music. Music can calm or excite our emotions, raise or lower our blood pressure, affect our respiration and brain cells. It can also destroy our hearing mechanism if played too loudly.[7]

In general, a decibel represents the difference the human ear can detect between the loudness of two sounds. Conversation in a relatively quiet setting ranges around 60 decibels, and the roar of traffic or sound of factory machinery is typically about 80 decibels. Anything above 80 is uncomfortable, and at 90, the experts start worrying about impact on health. A food blender, for example, is 93 decibels, and a motorcycle reving up, 110. Loud noise and noise that may be soft but irritating can produce harmful effects physically and mentally.[8] If you doubt the effect of sound on your body, just consider how you felt when someone slammed a door unexpectedly or a teacher scratched chalk on the blackboard.

Hearing loss is one of the most difficult sensory losses to tolerate, since it affects verbal communication, essential for social and environmental well-being. The stress of not hearing well also causes mental irritation and, at times, withdrawal and depression.

Fifty percent of those over age 65 suffer from some form of hearing impairment. This problem usually begins about age 20 and has been estimated to affect as many as 66 percent of the people over age 80.

Loss of hearing is not a normal part of aging, however, because in less industrialized, quieter societies, hearing is as keen at 75 years as at 17 years.[9] It has been reported a number of times that the popularity of loud rock and roll music has resulted in significant loss of hearing in many young people. It is most unwise for anyone to have music blasting through headphones, a common custom today. It can be not only painful, but cause permanent damage to your ability to hear and understand.

Sounds follow two paths to the brain: one to the auditory center on the side of the brain, where it is perceived and interpreted, the other to the base of the brain, where the control center for the autonomic nervous system lies. The autonomic nervous system involves the functions of the respiratory, circulatory, digestive, and urogenital systems, as well as the action of glands and the involuntary muscles in the skin. Just remember how you feel when a loud noise startles you. Your heart beats faster, you "catch your breath," and your stomach "knots." That would be a strong response to a startling noise, but even sounds to which you have become habituated and relatively oblivious may still provoke a physical "fight or flight" response —an increase in heart rate and blood pressure, constriction of the small blood vessels in the extremities, and release of the stress-related adrenal hormones. The auditory system even has an effect on the frontal lobe, which is involved in personality and intellectual function. Failure in the auditory pathways is believed by some to be the core defect in schizophrenia.

Scientists are studying how the brain "hears" by use of evoked potentials, measurements of the electrical output of the brain in response to a stimulus. It is an electrical measurement like voltage in an electrical line. Signal transmission is called the *potential.* To measure the current, a stimulus must be used to "evoke" it, such as a click or flashing light.

A fraction of a second after a person hears a click, for example, electrodes on the scalp can begin detecting the transmission of the "sound" from the ear, through the brain stem, and into the upper brain. The first component of the tracing is generated near the inner ear; components two through five arise in different regions of the brain stem. Where the signals go after that is still controversial, but it is known that by the time ten milliseconds have elapsed, the electrical response has probably reached the cerebral cortex.

In experiments at the University of Maryland, researchers played tones into the right ears of subjects and evoked an electrical brain-signal response on the right side of their brains. When the researchers again played the tone into the subjects' right ears but asked the subjects to count the tones in the left ear, the evoked electrical activity appeared on the left side of the brain.

While this work is far from completely accepted, it

seems to show that consciously making an effort to identify various stimuli can stimulate different areas of the brain.

In the meantime, it is up to you to protect your hearing by avoiding loud and/or irritating noise and by having any ear infections treated promptly. If you are constantly saying "What? What?" to people, you should have your hearing tested. There is no shame in augmenting your hearing with an aid, any more than there is to improving your vision with glasses.

The following are a few exercises for those hearing centers in your brain.

Talk Like the Animals

You'll probably want to do this while no one is around or else with someone who wants to perform too.

Imitate as many animal sounds as you can—dog, cat, tiger, coyote, bird, and so on into a tape recorder. The next day, play back the tape and try to identify which animals you were imitating.

Then make another tape, this time imitation of common noises in your environment, such as your car, the telephone, the bell, and repeat the procedure.

Music and Mood

Music—pleasant sounds—can have a profound effect on mood, as we have pointed out.

Leo Shatin, Ph.D., formerly professor of clinical psychology at the Mount Sinai School of Medicine in New York City and a researcher in music psychology, tested the mood-altering effects of music in a group-therapy setting: "We found that with slow, sad music people interacted less frequently. When someone finally did speak, it was usually with anger or hostility. Upbeat, cheerful songs, on the other hand, had people talking more and in a more friendly way."

Mood altering through music seems quite logical, according to Shelley Katsh, a certified music therapist. The theory: Certain musical abilities—singing, for example—are thought to be located on the same side of the brain, the right, as are our feelings and emotions.

Find That Beat
• Go over your tapes or records and choose a happy, fast-paced song; a slow, quiet one; and a moody, melancholy one.

Now, identify your mood. Are you agitated and nervous? If so, start out with the fast-paced music, the "jumping sound," and gradually change the records or tapes until you have serene, calm music playing.

Are you depressed or sluggish? Start with the slow, moody music and gradually change to light, happy music. You'll be surprised at how the music changes your mood.

• Do not listen to music for more than 20 minutes at a time, because it can fatigue your senses.

• Do not listen to music while you are trying to do a difficult intellectual task. It will interfere.

• Use music to lull you to sleep.

• Use music to create a romantic interlude. Usually, the music that was popular during the teenage years of the one you are trying to put in a romantic mood is the music to play.

Hear the News?—Increase Your Perception
Just as you can train your muscles to perform better, so too you can increase your auditory perception.

Get a news program or talk show on your radio, and turn the volume all the way down. Then draw a straight line on a piece of paper with your dominant hand.

Place the point of your pencil at the beginning of the line. With your nondominant hand, slowly turn the volume knob up at the same time you very, very slowly move the point of the pencil along the line. As soon as you can understand what is being said on the radio, make a mark on the line.

Keep repeating the process, trying to make the mark on the line earlier each time. This exercise is aimed at sharpening your hearing and your concentration. It would be beneficial to do it every day, but it should be done at least once a week.

THE SWEET SMELL OF STIMULATION

Gourmets may be proud of their sense of taste, yet taste is mostly smell. The senses of taste and smell are inextricably interconnected.

Our sense of taste is powerful. We can identify quinine, for instance, in as little as one part per billion solution, but taste pales next to our amazing ability to smell. We can detect an unlimited number of odors, some from far away and in dilutions as weak as one part in several billion parts of air. Arabs supposedly can smell a campfire 30 miles across a breezeless desert.

Everything has an odor to some degree, but particles for either taste or smell must be soluble. This is a throwback to our ancestral life in the sea when smell and taste were one. Sugar has no taste on a dry tongue, just as the scent of roses would go unnoticed in a dry nose.

The importance of each sense varies with each species. Birds, for instance, are said to rely very little on olfaction and depend mainly on sight and sound, while insects and the majority of mammals are dependent on their sense of smell. Until recently, most humans were reluctant to admit that they were affected physiologically and psychologically by what they smelled.

In 1959, researchers coined the word *pheromone*—from the Greek "pherein," meaning to carry, and "horman," meaning to excite or stimulate—to describe certain odors produced by the glands of animals. *Hormones,* the secretions of glands, also are named from "horman" because they "arouse to action." The difference between pheromones and hormones, however, is that hormones are secreted by an animal's own glands into its own bloodstream and affects the animal's own body and behavior. Pheromones, on the other hand, are also secreted by an animal's glands but are carried through the air to affect the body and behavior of another animal. You only have to have the experience of owning a female cat or dog in heat to know the power of a sexual pheromone. Male animals from near and far arrive at your door, frenzied by the female scent.

Though we may wish to deny it, we humans are manipulated by smells just as the butterfly, the salmon, and the ape. There are many scientists who now maintain that we emanate sexual scents and that "love at first sight" is really "love at first scent."

Our human olfactory cells are identical in construction to those of all other creatures from one end of the animal kingdom to the other. And while we may not be as good at smelling as the bloodhound or the shark, our sense of smell is pretty remarkable normally and when fully developed, astounding. One society matron, who wished to remain anonymous, amazed scientists in the 1940s with her ability to identify smells. She could report who last slept on a newly laundered pillowcase and was able to match coats in a closet to guests at a party by scent alone.

When we smell a perfume, for example, we smell the molecules of scent that have drifted to our noses. The odor molecules are inhaled with the air and dissolved on the wet film of mucus in our noses, and information about the molecules is relayed by sensory cells high in each nasal passage to the olfactory bulb, where it is sent along tracts in the olfactory lobe to the brain. We then realize within a thousandth of a second that the person is wearing a particular scent.[10] But how is the message encoded and delivered to the brain? How does the nose select one molecule over another, enabling one scent to overcome another? Why is the filing system of scent memories so efficient and apparently indestructible that we never forget what we have smelled, once the scent has been identified?

The incredibly specialized odor sensory cells, located high up in an inaccessible place at the top of each nasal passage, are pigmented yellow or brownish yellow, which distinguish them from the ordinary cells of the nose. In humans, they occupy an area about the size of a dime, whereas the smell sensory area in dogs and rabbits is about the size of a handkerchief.

Neuroanatomists have found the olfactory system unique because instead of going through the thalamus— that large area of brain just above the brain stem which acts as a relay station for the other senses to the neocortex —the olfactory cells send their signals directly to the brain area formerly called the rhinencephalon (from the Greek for "nose brain"). At one time this area—which is considered the oldest in evolutionary terms—was believed to deal only with smell. More than 30 years ago, however, anatomists found that this so-called nose brain also deals with the regulation of motor activities and the primitive drives of sex, hunger, and thirst. Therefore, the term *rhinencephalon* was changed to *limbic system,* derived from the limbus, or border, rimming the cortex of the brain.

Stimulation of the olfactory bulb shoots electrical signals to an almond-shaped area known as the *amygdala.* This part of the limbic system is concerned with visceral and behavioral mechanisms, particularly those associated with sensory and sexual functions. These signals are then relayed from the amygdala to the brain stem, the "turnpike" that contains the interconnections between brain and body. Therefore, the electrical stimulation involved in smelling directly affects the digestive and sexual systems and emotional behavior. Destruction of the amygdala area has resulted in a loss of fear and rage reactions, an increase in sexual activity, excessive eating, and severe deficiencies in memory.[11]

In 1937, Japanese researchers first reported there was electrical activity in sensory cells of the nose and in the brain when an odor stimulus occurred. It was not until the 1940s and 1950s that such electrical pulses were measured systematically as to strength, duration, and quality. The brain's electrical response to an odor appears to be indistinguishable from that correlated with emotional behavior. Since olfactory signals are sent to the amygdala area, it is easy to see how what we smell affects our emotions and our sex and hunger drives.

There are many conflicting opinions among researchers as to how the brain identifies smells. Some maintain that the olfactory bulb has been mapped for specific odors. For example, the inhalation of fruity scents activates the front part of the bulb, while solvents such as benzene stimulate preferentially the back part of the bulb.

A unique and as yet unexplained phenomenon of smell is that of adaptation. You know that no matter how strong an odor is when you enter a room, you become unaware of it or "blind" to it after a few minutes. When subjects are tested for recognition of various odors, a pause of at least 30 to 60 seconds has to be taken between each stimulation before an odor can be recognized. It has also been shown that prior exposure to one odorant will decrease the sensitivity to another. A higher concentration of the second scent is therefore required before the sniffer can identify it.

When scientists record the electrical activity that smelling an odor causes in the olfactory bulb, they find that even though the subjects can no longer detect the odor—say, of pine—the electrical signals continue unabated in their brains. In other words, the physical stimulus—the pine odor—still is at work but the subject is no longer aware of the scent.

Why is there adaptation? No one knows for certain, but some theorize that it is somehow involved in the protection of respiration. Perhaps we would stop breathing, or be unable to concentrate, if we were constantly aware of an odor. Or perhaps our other senses would be overpowered by our concentration on odor.

We influence our own behavior and the behavior of others with both natural and synthetic smells, often subconsciously. More and more research is being done in an attempt to understand this link between odors and behaviors. It is obvious that reactions to a specific smell are spontaneous and immediate. The sudden appearance of an odor can cause measurable changes in the resistance of the skin of a person, quite similar to that which takes place if he or she is suddenly startled.

When an odor is pleasant, there is a relaxation of the facial muscles, smiling, a pleasant tone of voice, laughing, nodding, opening of the mouth, and deeper respiration. When an odor is unpleasant, there is a turning away of the head and sometimes the entire body. The head may be jerked back, the nose wrinkled, and the upper lips raised.

Association with experience may play a part in determining such reactions, since odors are so closely linked to emotions and memory. Coloring may also affect the sense of pleasantness and unpleasantness. Green coffee would not smell as good as brown, and black strawberries would not seem as fragrant as red.

Manufacturers have made "new car smells" to make us think better of used cars, and the scent of bread baking is deliberately wafted into the street so that pedestrians will be enticed into a bakery. Using the scent of flowers and various animals to cover our own human scents is a multibillion-dollar industry. We are all led around by our noses.

Making Scent Associations
Take a pad and pencil and write down in a column your four favorite smells. Now write down your four most disliked smells.

Next to each smell, write your associations with those smells. The smell of baking bread, for example, might remind you of the warmth of your mother's kitchen on Sunday morning. Then write down whatever you associate with the bad smells.

After you have completed the list and associations, read it. It will give you a great deal of insight into your emotional history and will also have stimulated the area of the brain involved with odor and emotions.

Stimulate Your Olfactory Nerves
Take six envelopes, six cotton swabs, and six small pieces of paper. Dip a swab—so that you get just a tiny drop of liquid on it—in vanilla. Write down "vanilla" on the piece of paper and slip the swab and the paper in an envelope.

Repeat the procedures with a swab dipped in ammonia cleaner, a cooking oil, water, alcohol, and vinegar.

Once the swabs with their identifications are in the envelopes, shuffle them.

Close your eyes, take a swab out of one envelope, and sniff it. Repeat for each envelope. (Allow a count of 60 between sniffs.) Write down the identification of scents in the order you sniffed them. Your best memory is your odor memory. Just by testing it, you are using the olfactory lobe of your brain.

Odors, as we have pointed out, have a great deal to do with emotions and behavior. Susan Schiffman, Ph.D., of Duke University, a researcher in olfaction, maintains that women in their twenties use odor to attract and in their thirties to define their territory; in their fifties as an antidepressant and in their sixties, as a stimulus.[12]

You can change your mood with pleasant scents. Oriental perfumes are sultry and sexy; fruity, classic florals and green blends are reminiscent of the garden; and woodsy or leather scents are thought to be masculine. Herbal scents are popular among those who want to feel healthy and clean, since they contain a medicinal note.

To stimulate your sense of smell, imitate the ancient Greeks, who brought the scent of nature indoors. The Greeks had living rooms that opened onto beautiful gardens, where the most fragrant plants were placed near the windows in the belief that the scents had a salutary effect on the occupants of the house. In medieval monasteries, also, the monks planted sweet-smelling herbs near infirmaries for the benefit of their patients.

Those lucky enough to have gardens should consider the scenting of their homes when planting them. Night-blooming flowers can be placed by bedroom windows and day-blooming plants by the kitchen and living room windows.

Those who live in apartments can bring all sorts of fragrant plants into their homes, not only for their beauty but to humidify, deodorize, and scent the air.

Lavender has been used for centuries on sheets to encourage peaceful sleep, and a room scented with roses has been used as a "tranquilizer."

A MATTER OF TASTE

If everything tasted alike, eating would be boring.

Food is taken into your mouth, the first part of your digestive tract. Your teeth crush food so that enzymes can break it down more easily, while saliva lubricates it to make it easier to swallow.

Your tongue has a complex system of muscles that enables it to move food around as you chew and then to mold the chewed food into a ball for swallowing. The surface of your tongue is covered with minute hairlike projections surrounded by tastebuds.

The tastebuds can distinguish four main types of flavor: sweet, salt, sour, and bitter. Tastebuds are designed to warn you about rotten food and to give you pleasure.

There is a preference for sweetness at birth, but there is a difference, perhaps genetic, perhaps learned, in the levels of sweetness people prefer as they mature.

The front of the tongue is the most convenient and most widely used for taste testing because it is readily accessible and contains very few sensory fibers other than taste.

Tastebuds do diminish as most people age. At age 70, the average person has fewer tastebuds than at age 30. And most researchers agree that all four basic tastes commonly decline: sweet, salty, and bitter usually after 50 years, and sour after 60 years.[13]

The lips are involved not only in processing food and drink for taste and nourishment, but are also important to touch. Why else would we kiss? By stimulating the nerve endings on your lips and tongue, you stimulate the brain areas that receive their messages. Stimulation of the senses, as we have pointed out, helps preserve and improve function and increase pleasure.

Lip Exercises—Puckers and Smiles
• Rip a piece of paper into inch-long shreds and scatter the pieces on a tabletop. Place a saucer and a straw on the tabletop. Pick up each piece of paper by sucking it up with the straw and holding it by suction until you can transfer it to the saucer.
• Take a cotton ball and blow it across the table.
• Practice sounding out *U, P, B, M, D, W.*
• Whistle a happy tune.
• Tuck your lips in over your teeth and grin.
• Relax your lips and then move them toward one ear and then toward the other.

- Smile as hard as you can.
- Alternate pursing and retracting your lips.
- Stick your tongue out as far as you can and then wag it from side to side.
- Lick your tongue all around your lips as if you just ate something absolutely delicious.

THE TONGUE—A MAP OF TASTE BUDS

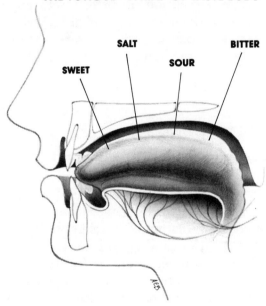

Taste Exercise

Take five envelopes and five cotton swabs and dip one swab in salt, another in lemon, another in sugar, another in vinegar, and the last in water.

Place the swabs in envelopes with their identifications written on small pieces of paper. Close your eyes.

With one hand, gently touch the top of your tongue with a swab and try to identify the taste. Repeat with the left rear side of your tongue and the right rear side. Write down what you believe the taste is. Wait 60 seconds and repeat with the next swab. Repeat the procedure for the remaining swabs.

Check your answers against the slips of paper in the envelopes.

Do this at least once a month and preferably once a week with a variety of taste samples of your choice.

Restaurant Guesser

To sharpen your perception of taste, try to guess the spices used in a particular restaurant dish. Write them down on a piece of paper and ask your server to take the paper to the chef and see how close you come. He or she will be flattered.

TOUCH ME IN THE MORNING

The surface of the skin is rich with sensory receptors designed to receive stimuli of heat, cold, touch, and pain. There are more than half a million sensory fibers from the skin entering the spinal cord.

The continuous stimulation of the skin by the external environment serves to maintain both sensory and motor fitness. The brain must receive sensory feedback from the skin in order to make such adjustments as may be called for in response to the information it receives. If your arm goes to sleep while you are lying on it, your skin will tell your brain to "move it."

Touching is perhaps our swiftest and most direct form of communication. When you touch someone, the millions of sensory receptors on the skin surface inform him or her not only about heat, cold, and pain but literally how you feel about that person.

Touch is a form of non-verbal communication that has been neglected compared to other kinds of expression. One reason is that it borders on being a taboo subject. How and whom you touch is carefully controlled. Yet most of us rarely go through the day without being touched or touching someone. Babies and older people who are not touched suffer not only emotional but physical decline. We need the stimulation of the touch of others. The manner in which the young of all mammals snuggle and cuddle against the body of the mother and against the bodies of their siblings or of any other introduced animal strongly suggests that cutaneous stimulation is an important biological need for both their physical and behavioral development. Almost every animal enjoys being stroked.[14]

We use touch to describe our feelings and our other sensations. If a patient has a chest pain and presses his chest with a clenched fist, this usually signifies that the pain is widespread and has a gripping quality. The pain from peptic ulcer is often closely localized and the patient describes it by delicately pointing to it with the tip of the index finger. If the pain is more or less superficial—what would normally be called soreness—the patient may lightly brush the surface of the skin with the outstretched tips of all five fingers.

The brain has a very large area reserved to receive messages from the various sensors in the skin. Nerve fibers conducting tactile impulses are generally of larger size than those associated with the other senses. In fact, human beings can lose their organs of sight, hearing, smell, and taste, but they cannot lose their skin and survive.

Touch Language
Touch is actually our swiftest form of communication. We can reach out and touch someone or we can draw back. We can slap when we are angry and caress when we are loving. Such gestures are obvious but you can also practice "reading" through your skin. Have someone lightly draw

with a finger or pencil on your back numbers and letters or even words—and try to identify the message.

Have You Hugged Your Pillow Today?

You can reach out and touch someone or some animal. If you are too shy or do not have a pet to stroke, adopt the Chinese custom. Buy a soft bolster, an elongated pillow, or just a large bed pillow. Almost everybody, including males in China, is given a pillow from the time of birth. These "holding" pillows (bolsters) are small for infants and "grow" with the child. The largest size is for adults. You can wrap your arms and legs around them. They are soft and filled with cotton. In the traditional Chinese bridal chamber, a bolster—just one—is placed in the middle of the bed.

Take a pillow to bed with you and cuddle it. The feeling of comfort you will receive will probably be due to your brain's release of its own tranquilizers, the endorphins, in response to the stimulation of your skin by your hugging of the pillow.

The Massage Is the Message

Many cultures have recognized that the "laying on" of hands is healing, relaxing, and sensual. If you have someone who will massage your skin with a favorite lotion, that is ideal. If not, you can massage yourself. Starting at your toes, and working your way up your body, including the arms and neck, to your face, massage gently while you are relaxed. Music played softly may help and so may a darkened room. At least once a week, or more often if you are very tense or feeling "blue," have a massage. Again, the stimulation your brain receives from stroking the skin is soothing because your brain responds to it by releasing its tranquilizing endorphins.

Touch Identification
Gather a variety of materials, such as a swatch of terry-cloth, a piece of velvet, cotton balls, feathers, and sandpaper. Again, put one of each material in an unmarked envelope. Shuffle the envelopes. Close your eyes and, with just the tip of your index finger, feel the material and write the identification down. If you have another person available, lie on your abdomen and have your partner lightly rub each material against your bare back while you try to identify it.

Some Like It Hot, But Not Too Hot

The upper limit of tolerable body temperatures in most land vertebrates is 104° to 122° F (40° to 50° C). Although excessive temperatures affect virtually every organ, the brain function appears to be especially vulnerable to heat. If the brain is kept cool, tolerance to elevated body temperature is extended. The temperature of the mammalian brain is determined by the rate of heat production of brain cells, the rate of blood flow through the brain, and the temperature of the blood supplying the brain. In addition, the temperature of the brain can be influenced by direct heat through the scalp or through the base of the skull. We cool ourselves by sweating on the face. Fanning your face causes the temperature of the brain to drop.

Temperature affects how well you think. The cognitive performance of six male Marines undergoing a 10-degree heat acclimatization regimen was assessed by giving them things to learn and by asking them to estimate the passage of time. Subjects performed controlled treadmill exercises in a heat acclimatization chamber at 33.3° F (4° C). Their performance was tested several times during the 155 minutes each day that they were exposed to heat. On the first day of heat exposure, their ability to estimate time fell below the ability they showed at moderate room temperature and so did their ability to learn. By the tenth day of heat exposure, all subjects demonstrated significant heat acclimatization. However, their learning tasks were still impaired and their time estimates were higher than during their first exposure to heat. These results suggest that learning new tasks may be difficult in a hot environment, even for partially acclimatized individuals.[15]

Many studies have shown that human beings seem to function best physically and mentally at 68° F (20° C) and 40 percent humidity. You should keep that in mind if you have a challenging mental task to perform. Yet, what may be comfortable for you may not be comfortable for others.

Temperature Test Yourself

Try to memorize one short passage from a book at 65° F (18.33° C); another at 70° F (21.11° C); and still another at 78° F (25.55° C). (This exercise requires a home thermostat.) Choose the temperature at which learning was easiest. It would be a good idea to repeat the test on another day, reversing the temperature factors, to make sure it was temperature and not fatigue that made the difference.

Take Your Temperature

Our brains are affected not only by the environmental temperature but by our internal temperature, which rises and falls in a 24-hour pattern. Your body temperature is probably highest in the late afternoon and lowest in the morning. Your brain will function best at certain times of the day that can be marked by how warm or cool your body is. At right is a chart to track your temperature, your cognition, and your mood at various times of the day.

Save four crossword puzzles from the daily newspaper or buy a puzzle book. Take your temperature as soon as

Time	Day 1			Day II			Day III			
	Temp-erature	Mood	Puzzle	Temp-erature	Mood	Puzzle	Temp-erature	Mood	Puzzle	Average Temperature
7 A.M.										
8 A.M.										
9 A.M.										
10 A.M.										
11 A.M.										
12 P.M.										
1 P.M.										
2 P.M.										
3 P.M.										
4 P.M.										
5 P.M.										
6 P.M.										
7 P.M.										
8 P.M.										
9 P.M.										
10 P.M.										
11 P.M.										
12 A.M.										
1 A.M.										
2 A.M.										
3 A.M.										

you wake up, mark it on the chart, note your mood, and then do as much of the puzzle as you can in ten minutes. Write down how much you finished—a quarter of it, a third, half, three-quarters, or all.

Take your temperature and do a puzzle at noon, at 5 P.M., and at 9 P.M. Record your temperature, mood, and how much of the puzzle you completed. The rest of the day and evening, record just your temperature and mood at various times. Repeat the process for the next two days.

By looking at the chart, you should be able to see the body temperature and the time of the day at which you function best. Keep this in mind and try to schedule your most challenging intellectual tasks at your peak time and your routine, automatic tasks at your low time.

BE SENSATIONAL AND FEEL BETTER

Your ability to sense your world inside and out is what makes you uniquely human and provides you with the pleasures of life. John Keats wrote to a friend in 1817, "O for a life of sensations rather than of thoughts." What the poet did not realize is that without sensations, there can be no thoughts, and without thoughts, there can be no sensations. Our ears, eyes, nose, mouth, and skin provide the information from the internal and external environment that is processed by our brains; and, in turn, our brains signal our organs about the meaning of what is being sensed.

By becoming more aware of the power of your senses, by performing the exercises in this chapter and the others in the book, you will help to increase and maintain the fitness of your brain.

3

Improving the Coordination of Brain, Muscle, and Nerve

Pick up a cup.

Do you realize the tremendous cooperation required between your brain, nerves, and muscles to accomplish that feat? Your brain had to send signals to your shoulder, arm, wrist, and fingers. Your elbow had to bend. You had to reach out. Your fingers had to close and grasp, feel the weight of the cup, and then lift it up in the right direction —all in a series of rapid, precisely coordinated movements. Then your fingers and arm had to send back a message to your brain, "Mission accomplished!"

You picked up that cup without thinking about it, and yet just the ability of your thumb and fingers to make a pinching movement is one of the major reasons you are prime among the primates and all other creatures on earth. Of course, if you had to figure out how to pick up a cup every time you did it, you wouldn't be able to concentrate on anything else. A large part of movement, therefore, is both involuntary and outside your consciousness.

Investigators have recently discovered that your brain has prerecorded instructions, a "computer program," for virtually every movement. These programs can be expanded in healthy people and recompiled in the brain-injured through stimulation either by "reentering" coordinated movements or by programmed electrical charges.[1-4]

The natural computer program for your hand is stored in an area specifically set aside for it in your cerebral cortex. Just as a writer wouldn't use an accounting program as much as he would a word-processing one, the brain allots more space to some data bases than to others. The more sensitive the surface of your body, the larger its "map" in the brain. Thus the amount of brain tissue that contains input from the hand is quite a bit larger than that for the entire surface of the back and the legs.

The way the hand inputs to the brain is consistent from one member of the same species to another. The brain's space allotted to the fingers takes up almost the entire area assigned to the hand, with relatively less cortex remaining to receive information from the palm. The area assigned to individual fingers varies greatly. It has no relation to the size of your hand. It has to do with the way you use your fingers.

Scientists now believe that you can increase the area of the brain assigned to your fingers by increasing your use of them.[5] This was demonstrated in monkeys who were trained to maintain continuous contact with a disc for about 15 seconds to obtain food. The disc was always available in the home cage and provided the only source of food. Moving the disc resulted in about two and a half hours of skin stimulation. The task required a high level of attentiveness. The experiment was conducted for several weeks. Detailed electrophysiological maps of the hand representation in the brain were studied before stimulation was begun and several months after the repetitive hand use had ended. Significant alteration of brain areas resulted from the heavy, behaviorally controlled hand use.

These studies reveal that "brain maps" for the fingers can be altered substantially in adult monkeys, a fact that

SPECIALIZED MOVEMENTS CONTROLLED BY THE BRAIN

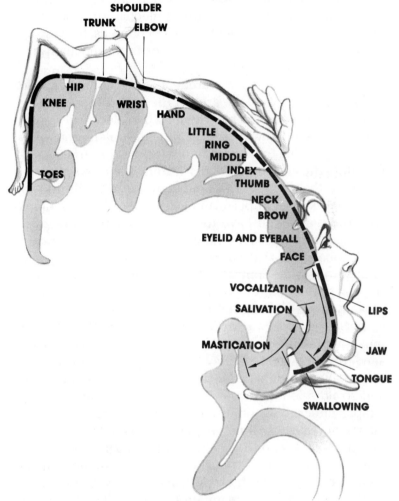

contradicts the widely held notion, the researchers said, that representational maps are strictly anatomically determined and are only subject to modification for a short while after birth. It also helps to explain the possible mechanisms underlying the acquisition of skill by practice, such as piano playing or the sport of tennis.[6]

Animal studies also show that when one programmed area is damaged or an in-putting mechanism, such as a finger, is not working, the brain can compensate for it by expanding the area assigned to other input mechanisms, such as the other fingers. For example, when researchers tested monkeys who had lost their fingers, the area in the cortex representing the lost digits were at first "silent" when electrical signals were recorded. However, over time, the silent zones became responsive to tactile stimulation of skin surfaces surrounding the amputated digits, leading the researchers to conclude that in an adult "brain maps" can be altered by use. That is why to perform at a superior level, such as with the piano, you have to practice, practice, practice!

No one knows exactly how the new maps are drawn, but it is believed that fibers running from the motor area of the brain to the spinal cord are organized in such a way that each small motor brain map, controlling a particular movement, is surrounded by a "fringe" of motor nerve cells that have only a partial influence on that particular movement. When the main "brain map" becomes damaged, the "fringe area" may eventually take over. If such shifts could be enhanced, then certainly many accident and stroke victims would benefit and so would healthy people undergoing brain changes due to aging. Recent efforts on the behalf of people with paralyzed limbs is proving that it is possible. When a limb is paralyzed, there is an interruption in transmission between the control center, the brain, and the outlying stations, the limbs.

Although textbooks maintain that neurological deficits that persist more than six months are permanent, researchers at the University of Massachusetts have been proving that those "downed wires" can be bypassed or reconnected to reestablish transmission of nerve signals. Professor Walter P. Kroll and his colleagues at the university have been using Functional Electrical Stimulation (FES) and reestablishing movement years after function has been been absent. Kroll, a professor of exercise science, said his most spectacular case was a 33-year-old man whose left arm had been paralyzed since he was 9. After treatment, the man was able to gain independent control of his fingers and to flex his elbow enough to feed himself.

Kroll, who began his research nearly two decades ago with a grant from the United States Army, said his aim at the beginning was to gain a better understanding of how the brain controls movement. He and his other researchers have now concluded that the human brain has computerlike "programs" for various movements. By analyzing those muscle signals with a computer as the unaffected limb is moved, they can imitate the muscle pattern with electronics. The muscle pattern developed from the unaffected limb is then fed to the muscles of the immobile limb by electrical stimulation.

The amount of movement recovered after FES treatments depends upon a number of factors, including the length of time the limb has been affected, severity of the muscle and nerve damage, and the general health of the individual. However, Kroll and his colleagues feel that they are finally able to communicate directly with the brain in "a language the brain understands."[7]

Increased understanding of the brain is rapidly being accumulated by neuroscientists. Old beliefs, such as the one about a lost brain function being irretrievable after six months, are being modified. Another is that the cerebellum is subservient to the cortex, the "thinking brain," for the highest level of movement coordination. It now appears that the situation is quite the reverse.

The coordination of the complicated signals that move your hands so that you can grasp a cup, pet a cat, or play the piano are processed by your cerebellum. The cerebellum is that part of the brain associated with coordination of muscles governing locomotion, posture, speech, and skilled movement. It lies at the back of your skull behind your brain stem and under the great hemispheres of your cerebrum. Its name is a Latin diminutive of *cerebrum* and means simply "lesser brain." It is much smaller than the cerebrum but looks like it. As in the cerebrum, the highest functions in the cerebellum are confined to the thin outer layer, which, like the cerebrum's, is folded and wrinkled to increase its area. The folds, in fact, are much deeper and more closely spaced than those of the cerebral cortex. If the cerebellum is split down the middle, the folds form a pattern that resembles a tree which medieval anatomists termed the "arbor vitae," or tree of life.

Test Your Cerebellum

• With your hands at your side, close your eyes and touch your nose with one index finger and then with the other. Do this four times.

• Place a string on the floor or follow a straight line and walk heel to toe along it.

• Stand by a wall or chair so you can catch yourself, if necessary. Close your eyes and try to balance on one foot for the count of 10.

• Lie on your back with eyes shut and both legs straight. Then lift one leg and put its heel on the knee of the other leg. Try this test four times with each heel.

In a month, after you've done the cerebellar exercises we describe later in this chapter, try these tests again. You may notice a difference.

The cerebellum is being studied intensively today because it seems especially vulnerable to age. Elderly people generally require more time to prepare for and carry out a movement, pace themselves poorly in tasks requiring continuous performance, and fail to adjust their movements to compensate for errors. Why? In the past, such changes were thought to be related to decreased muscle strength or to the accumulation of fat with age. Now a National Institute on Aging–supported study of old animals suggests that changes in the brain may be responsible for many of the disturbances in movement that are seen in animals. Aged rats move their limbs less vigorously during prolonged exercise than do young adult rats. These movement disorders are strikingly similar to those seen in young adult rats with damaged dopamine-producing brain areas. There is evidence that the impaired function of aged rats can be reversed by administration of the amino acid L-dopa. It has long been known that dopamine, containing neurons of the brain, plays a critical role in movement, but recent research seems to indicate that dopamine may also affect the movement problems of healthy aged populations.[8]

Floyd Bloom, Ph.D., director of the Division of Preclinical Neuroscience and Endocrinology, Scripps Clinic and Research Foundation, in California, and his colleagues, for example, studied Purkinje neurons, the large output cells of the cerebellum. Each of the millions of Purkinjes constantly receives a variety of incoming electrical signals, carrying the information about the position of the body and the movements it must make.

Dr. Bloom found that as rats age, an increasing proportion of their Purkinje cells fire abnormally and the total number of these cells declines. Moreover, the loss of Purkinje cells in each animal seems to be closely linked to the loss of muscular coordination. The fewer the cells, the greater the lack of balance.

The studies also indicate that many Purkinje cells tend to wither in old age. They lose some of their dendrites and the treelike branches where incoming information is received and so are less able to pick up and process certain types of incoming information.[9]

Coordination is affected, including manual dexterity. Dr. Mark Williams, M.D., assistant professor of medicine at the University of Rochester, maintains that timing a person's manual dexterity is much more accurate than traditional tests for predicting his or her need for long-term care. Traditional tests include questions to assess an individual's alertness and tests to determine whether or not the person can perform the routine tasks of daily living.

Williams says that it must be determined why a person's speed of hand function is below a certain critical level. The loss of manual dexterity may be due to arthritis, a thyroid problem, or to medication and may be improved with simple treatment. If, however, the loss is caused by a decline in the workings of the brain, then greater measures must be taken to increase the functioning of its motor centers or to make up for the deficit by other means.[10]

What can you do to enhance the function of your cerebellum?

Cerebellar stimulation—using coordinated movement —is one answer. Learning motor skills can, again, be compared to programming a computer. You can see a baby programming the cerebellum when you put a cup on his or her high-chair tray. The first time the baby tries to pick it up, the hands oscillate and knock the cup off. Presently, the cerebellum learns to judge how far to move the hand, how much to expand or contract the grasp.

In the adult, there is calculation of other fine measurements. For example, in tennis, the ball is hit toward you. You instantly have to determine:
- How fast is it coming?
- Where should the racket be when it gets here?
- Do I need to move?
- What angle should I use?

When you become expert at tennis, your cerebellum

plugs in the almost infinitely modifiable program for playing in a smoothly perfected manner.

You can be quite certain that Olympic athletes have cerebellums that operate with rapid communication between nerve cells and muscles. Because they constantly repeat their movements, their actions have become semiautomatic. If the cerebellum is damaged, however, through disease or injury, or infrequently challenged, one may be forced to consciously think through every fine movement, and those movements would not be as well executed as if they were done semiautomatically.

You may not become an Olympic athlete if the cerebellum with which you were born is not in top condition. But no matter what your age, you can improve what you have, often to a marked degree. Even if your competitor was born with a better cerebellum, motivation—that as yet unexplained phenomenon—can put you further ahead. It takes motivation and constant dedicated practice to improve.

One of the fundamental functions of the cerebellum is to help us learn and remember new movements, such as playing the piano. This suggests that the ability of the motor system to adapt to learning special movements may be significant in cases where damage to other parts of the brain requires reorganization. Under these circumstances the cerebellum may modify nerve function to compensate for impairment in the damaged parts of the brain.[11]

The cerebellum is vital to balance and movement, although the inner ear and other central nervous system components are also involved. The following exercises will help you improve balance and coordination.

The Old Book-on-Head Routine
Place a book on your head and walk forward along a

straight line. You can place a string on the floor or follow a floor board or rug pattern, just as long as you follow a straight line, heel to toe, heel to toe.

Now, instead of walking forward along the line, walk sideways, stepping with your left foot and bringing your right to it. Then, when you reach the end of the line, go back, stepping with your right foot and bringing your left foot to it, still balancing the book on your head.

Repeat both heel-to-toe walking and side-stepping with the book on your head, but sing a song—any song—as you do it.

Backward Pickup

Place an object, such as a book or a can of food, on the floor. Walk 20 paces away. Make sure there are no objects to trip over and then walk backward without looking back while singing any song you choose. Bend to pick up the object at the place you believe it is.

Repeat this exercise three times, each time walking farther away and then back, but always singing something as you walk backward. This is to develop your sense of timing and hand-eye coordination.

Stork Balance

Do not do this exercise if you have difficulty with your balance or you have a condition that might be affected if you fall. As a safety precaution, stand near a wall or chair so that if you feel like falling, you can catch yourself.

• Center yourself and consciously balance on both feet. Close your eyes and count to three.

• Balance on your right foot, with your eyes still closed, to the count of three.

• Balance on your left foot, with your eyes still closed, and count to three.

- Open your eyes. Center yourself consciously on your two feet and count to five.
- With your eyes open, balance on your right foot, with your left foot hooked behind your right knee, and count to three.
- Center yourself on both feet and count to three.
- Balance yourself on your right foot while holding your left foot in your hand and count to three.
- Assume various kinds of body positions—use your imagination—while balancing on one foot. You might pretend to be the Statue of Liberty or an ostrich. Count to three.

Each day, try to increase the count while you balance with any of the above stances until you can get to 15 while standing on one foot with your eyes closed.

Blanket Roll
Spread a blanket on the floor or on your bed and, with one hand over your head, roll to the right and then to the left. Roll right three times and left three times. Then roll yourself in the blanket with your head sticking out. This exercise helps you control your body while it is moving.

Table Topping
Lean over a table or desk with your feet on the floor and curl your fingers around the far edge of the table. Bend one knee and lift your bent leg toward the ceiling; do not allow your knee to turn out. Lift ten times. Repeat for the other leg.

Table topping will help to keep the communication going between your legs and your brain via your spine. Of course, don't do it if you have a physical condition that might cause you pain or injury while performing it.

Shrug It Off
In a standing position, shrug your shoulders forward, up, down, and back. Your chest should elevate. Repeat ten times. This not only exercises control over your shoulders but helps relax tension that might interfere with performance.

Body-Movement Exercises for the Cerebellum

Square dancing is one of the best. You are not only executing movement to music, you are following the directions of the caller. Any dancing, however, is good for your cerebellum.

Simon Sez, that children's game where you imitate the leader and try to avoid following directions when "Simon Sez" is not spoken, is good for the same reasons that square dancing is beneficial. You have to pay attention, follow directions, and execute patterned moves.

Charades. In this game you try to describe a "saying" or "object" to others strictly by pantomime. Charades is excellent for your cerebellum, as well as the right side of your brain, because it employs body control as a substitute for speech.

Pat Yourself on the Head. Another child's game that can benefit your cerebellum is tapping the top of your head with one hand and rubbing your stomach with the other. Remember that? Do it for the count of 20 and then reverse your hands and repeat for the count of 20. Do it as often as you can.

Handy Movements—Dexterity Exercises
The fine, coordinated movement of the fingers and hands
depends a great deal on the cerebellum. By carefully following the exercises below, you can increase your dexterity.

Coin Stacker. Take 100 pennies or dimes and stack
them as high as you can. You might also try stacking coins
of different denominations, but this requires precise
placement.

Saucey Saucer. Take a saucer or ashtray. Dump some
coins and/or buttons on the tabletop; then pick up and
place as many of them in the dish as fast as you can—
within 30 seconds.

Tweezer Pickup. Take a tweezer and several dozen
loose straight pins. Put the pins on the table. Pick them
up with the tweezer one at a time and place them in a
saucer or ashtray. Place as many as you can within a count
of 30. Keep trying to better the number you can place in
the dish each time you try the exercise.

Hand-Eye Exercises
The extraordinary coordination between the hand and
the eye involves fine movement. The following exercises
will help strengthen the pathways.

• Connect the circles in order and as quickly as you can without lifting your pencil from the paper.

• Connect the circles with a pencil line, but this time alternate between numbers and letters, keeping both in sequence.

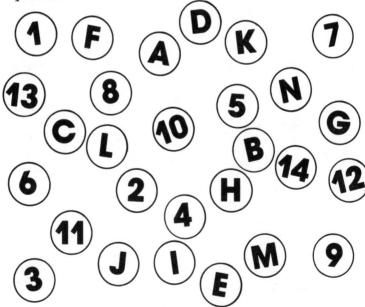

The Amazing Maze. Draw a path with your pencil without lifting it from the paper and without crossing a line from beginning to end.

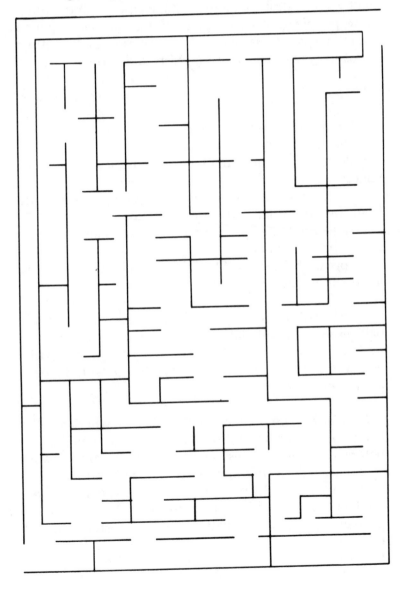

Cut It Out. Take a scissors and cut out figures or objects from magazines or newspapers. Try to follow the outline as closely as possible. If you have no scissors available or don't want to destroy the page, take a pencil and outline all the people or objects without lifting your pen or pencil from the page. Remember to stick as closely to the outline as possible, with all the little twists and turns.

Finger Fun. This is excellent for improving dexterity.
- Bend one finger at a time.
- Shake one finger at a time.
- Place your hands on a table and drum and tap your fingers.
- Move each finger in a half circle in sequence starting from the little finger on your left hand.
- Hold your fingers together and extend and separate them one at a time.
- Spread the fingers of both hands and touch fingers to fingers in a clapping motion.

Put the Squeeze On. Take a box or basket and put in a ball, a sponge, a soft cloth, and a piece of elastic (the kind sold in the variety store to repair undergarments). While you watch TV, without looking at the basket, squeeze and/or pull each item several times.

Play Jacks. The popular children's game where a ball is tossed in the air and a metal double cross is picked up before the ball bounces is one of the best exercises for your cerebellum. It requires hand speed and coordination. You start out by picking up one jack at a time before the ball bounces, and then you increase the number you pick up until you can gather them all before the ball bounces.

Bowling and baseball are two other recreational pursuits that are very good for your cerebellum. In bowling, you have to coordinate your movements and aim the ball at a distant pin. In baseball, you have to time your swing to hit the ball.

You know from experience that practice improves performance. Now prove it again by doing these brain builders for your cerebellum.

4

Aerobics for the Brain

You know that physical exercise can improve your physical fitness. How about your mental fitness?

There is controversy over exactly why and how physical exercise improves cognition, but there is agreement that it can be highly beneficial. Cognition is the quality of *knowing*. It includes perceiving, recognizing, conceiving, judging, sensing, reasoning, and imagination.

As we get older, the reflex time required to prepare and carry out purposeful movement increases. The physiologic response of reduced brain-wave frequency can be seen on the electroencephalograph. Slower electrical conduction along nerve pathways and slower reaction time do affect mental functions such as intellect, memory, attention, and perception.

In the recent past, declines in reaction times or voluntary movements were thought to be due to decreased muscle strength or to accumulation of fat within the body. Now, researchers believe that these changes are largely due to modifications in the central nervous system.

One theory is that some decline in function results from an insufficient supply of oxygen to the brain. It has been determined at the National Institute on Aging's Baltimore Gerontology Research Center that there is a drop in the amount of oxygen taken in by the lungs as we age. The circulating blood of a 20-year-old man, the NIA studies show, will take up, on the average, almost 4 liters of oxygen per minute. The circulating blood of a 75-year-old will take up only 1.5 liters per minute.

Reduced oxygen levels have been shown to cause a decline in the following neurotransmitter chemicals with which the brain's nerves communicate:

• *Dopamine.* A neurotransmitter present in high concentrations in the brain, it has been proven in animal studies to be necessary for initiating fast movements and to be affected by vigorous exercise.[1]

• *Norepinephrine* (noradrenaline). A hormone from the adrenal gland (just above the kidneys), it stimulates nerve cells, particularly those of smooth muscles, and constricts blood vessels.

• *Serotonin.* A blood-vessel constrictor present in high concentrations in the brain, it inhibits secretions in the digestive tract and stimulates smooth muscles.

Each of these neurotransmitters has been correlated with human behavior—and the function of each declines with age.

Neurons that release these chemical messengers are in the base of the brain around the reticular formation, a structure highly involved in arousal and attention. Those nerves that secrete norepinephrine or serotonin reach to the hypothalamus, the limbic system, and other structures, while the nerves producing dopamine project primarily to the basal ganglia. The basal ganglia, limbic system, and hypothalamus play a role in motor behaviors and in emotional and motivational states. Sleep, pleasure, eating, reproductive behavior, and stress-related aggression all emanate from this area.

In one classic experiment, older rats housed in environments that provided for increased sensory and motor stimulation were shown to have increased size and complexity of nerve networks. The area of transmission of the nerve chemicals dopamine, norepinephrine, and serotonin were larger than that of rats in an ordinary environment. The researchers concluded that the changes may have occurred because of increased oxygenation of the brain tissues.[2]

It has been known for a long time that in patients with Parkinsonism—which has been called the "stalking horse" of senescence—there is insufficient dopamine in the areas of the brain associated with movement. Hence, victims of Parkinsonism have difficulty moving and may lose their balance in a manner we associate with the very, very old.

There is substantial evidence that movement, sensory stimulation, and even "thinking" result in an immediate increase of blood flow to the brain. The physical activities associated with an exercise program, in addition to improving the intake and use of oxygen aerobic efficiency, may, in humans, provide sufficient brain stimulation to promote physical changes in the brain and improve its function.[3]

Testing with human subjects seems to bear this out.

Studies have shown that the reaction times of men who have maintained an active participation in physical activities such as racquet sports and running were significantly faster than those of age-matched sedentary men and little different from response times of much younger sedentary subjects.[4] Highly physically fit older individuals scored higher on tests of fluid intelligence (the functioning of neurological structures) and memory retention than did less fit subjects.[5]

But did the better performance of physically fit older individuals reflect a predisposition for superiority in both athletic and cognitive abilities, or did their physical activity per se have the beneficial effect on their central nervous system function?

If the latter were true, then could the central nervous system function of older people be significantly improved with a program of physical activity even though they have maintained a sedentary lifestyle for many years? Would aerobic exercises that emphasize increasing the oxygen in the muscles for strength and flexibility also help the brain?

There have been a number of studies to determine whether aerobic physical activity may really improve brain function.

In one study, sedentary individuals between 55 and 70 years of age were enlisted in a four-month aerobic exercise conditioning program. They were compared to two age-matched control groups:

1. Those trained with strength and flexibility exercises but not with exercises that increased oxygen intake.
2. Those not engaged in any supervised exercise program.

The aerobically trained subjects showed significantly greater improvement on neuropsychological tests and did better than either control group. The researchers concluded that the aerobic exercises promoted increased brain metabolism with a resultant improvement in neuropsychological test scores.[6]

In another study, researchers at Purdue University in Indiana enlisted 70 members of the faculty and business community between the ages of 24 and 68 to participate in a four-month physical fitness program.[7] The subjects were divided into the following groups:

High-fit young.
High-fit old.
Low-fit young.
Low-fit old.

Each group was given 90-minute exercise sessions a week, beginning with warm-up calisthenics and then progressive running and self-selected recreational activities.

There was a marked improvement in fluid intelligence in all groups, the researchers said. Fluid intelligence, which is discussed more thoroughly in Chapter 6, is the functioning of the neurological structures and is believed to decline with age unless some type of intervention takes place. The researchers found that regardless of age, the high-fit group had a significantly higher total fluid intelligence score than the low-fit group.

The researchers noted that oxygen itself may not play the major role in improved cerebral functioning, but it may affect the changes in brain chemistry that do.

The observed beneficial results of exercise—including its antidepressant effects—have been attributed to the release of endorphins, neurotransmitters that cause feelings of euphoria. The morphinelike neurotransmitters are released by the brain and pituitary gland. Increased beta-endorphin levels during exercise are thought to cause the phenomenon known as "runner's high" and may explain why runners become addicted to the sport and are depressed if they miss a day. The beta-endorphins also increase tolerance to pain, which may also explain why some people run despite pulled muscles, chest discomfort, and other agonies.

A study conducted by Dr. Daniel B. Carr, of Massachusetts General Hospital, and other researchers revealed that levels of beta-endorphin rose dramatically in the blood of nonathletes while exercising and that these levels increased even higher with regular training.[8]

There is no doubt that there is a hormonal effect from running, since persistent and vigorous exercise by female runners has delayed or eliminated their menstruation. It makes sense that fluctuations in the intensity of nerve communication caused by exercise can have a marked influence on the function of the nervous system. A popular hypothesis is that exercise improves the body's adaptation to emotional stress by increasing the efficiency of the adrenal glands, which release "fight or flight" chemicals such as norepinephrine in response to stress. You can see, therefore, how exercise that may affect the brain by increasing blood flow, oxygen, and metabolism could affect mood as well as cognition.[9]

There are those, however, who maintain that increased oxygen to the brain or changes in the neurochemistry of the brain are not the cause of the improved mental functioning as reported in experiments such as the one performed by Dr. Carr. Some researchers theorize that the reason you "feel better" when you exercise is because you have enhanced feelings of self-worth and decreased psychological stress. Some investigators think that the results are due to distraction from worry during exercise and that the social interaction and the feelings of mastery or accomplishment are the reasons people's mental functions seem to improve.[10] The actual result may be a combination of both theories—but beneficial in any case.

In an effort to determine just how exercise does affect mood, researchers studied 64 subjects prior to and after either vigorous exercise or a hobby class. In general, the results support the claim that physical activity is associated with changes in mood and mental functioning. Although significant changes on several variables were also observed in the hobby group, the magnitude of changes from pre- to post-testing was greater for the exercise group.[11]

Among the parameters measured were anxiety, depression, self-confidence, adjustment, work efficiency, and sleep behavior. The hobby classes included painting, photography, typing, auto mechanics, and nutrition courses. The exercise class involved 45 minutes of jogging and various other physical activities.

All took place between 6:30 and 7:30 P.M. to remove daily mood variations. The study showed that the exercise group felt more elated, less apprehensive, less serious, and less engaged in thought. They were also less fatigued and less unhappy following exercise. Their scores on the profile of mood scale revealed they also felt less anxious, less depressed, and less angry. And they had increased alertness and physical well-being.

The explanation as to why alertness is increased by exercise may be found in experiments in which ten men and eight women, aged 19 to 24, were exercised to the point of exhaustion by researchers at New Mexico State University. After the volunteers had run on treadmills, their brain waves were recorded and they underwent tests of their perceptual and motor skills. The investigators found that there was significantly higher activity in the left hemisphere of the brain than in the right in the subjects, and that this implied a more analytical mode of thinking due to the exercise.[12]

Exercises—particularly aerobic routines that increase the oxygen to your brain and stimulate the release of beneficial neurotransmitters—are good for your brain. If you do the following exercises faithfully, you should feel better and think better within three weeks.

Brain Breathing

We breathe 20,000 times a day, but do we breathe well enough to supply our brains with sufficient oxygen? The single best indicator of fitness, according to many exercise physiologists, is how easily the body takes in and uses oxygen during work performed on a bicycle or treadmill. The more physically fit, the better the oxygen metabolism.

If you don't believe your breathing can immediately affect your brain, take ten rapid deep breaths. It should make you feel light-headed because you have deliberately lowered the carbon dioxide in your blood.

The yogis have always emphasized proper breathing as a means of controlling body processes, including the brain and its by-product, emotions.

How efficiently do you breathe?

Test your respiratory efficiency. Lie down. Place your left hand on your lower abdomen and your right hand on your chest, just below your throat. Take several deep breaths as you would ordinarily, but try to exhale more deeply than usual. As you repeat this, you'll probably notice that when you exhale, your abdomen doesn't move much. Your chest is doing most of the work. This is called "paradoxical breathing" because it produces the opposite of what it should. During exhalation, your diaphragm tightens and drops down, expanding the lungs. Upon inhaling, your diaphragm relaxes and is pushed up by the muscular contractions of the abdominal wall, thereby reducing lung volume. Your respiratory system works against itself. Paradoxical breathing often follows breath-holding, which occurs when you try something new, are startled, or shift your attention. This is illustrated by the following:

1. Stand up quickly and then sit down again.
2. Snap your fingers about once a second. With each snap, shift your eyes so that with one snap you look to the extreme right and the next snap, to the extreme left. Repeat about 10 to 15 times.

What happened to your breath pattern? Didn't you hold your breath and then breathe shallowly with your chest? Such respiration is inefficient and tension-producing.

Belly breathing—using your abdominal muscles during inhalation—is a relaxed method of breathing and conserves energy.[13]

Try it. Start by sticking out your stomach and pushing

it against your left hand. Then inhale up into your chest, pushing it against your right hand. Exhale even a bit more. Repeat this slowly, making your breathing rhythmic. Now, breathe into your left hand and then into your right, and then exhale very deeply. Do it to a slow count of 8.

The more you practice belly breathing, the more automatic it should become. You'll find yourself able to think better and move better and even play sports better because belly breathing is an efficient way of taking in oxygen and getting rid of the waste product, carbon dioxide. And, when facing a stressful situation, if you increase and deepen your belly breathing, you'll send out the calming neurotransmitters from your brain and reduce the level of the excitatory ones.

Skull Shining. This is what yogis call this exercise because it brings a "radiant brightness" to your head. While sitting or standing, curl your lips over your teeth, leaving just a slit of your mouth open. Inhale deeply through your nose. Exhale forcefuly through the slit between your lips in a series of short, distinct bursts of air. After completely exhaling, take several relaxed breaths and repeat once or twice more.

Breath Relaxer. This exercise will relax you and allow you to breathe more efficiently as it counteracts your "tightness" or stress. It is great to do while you are standing impatiently in line.

Stand with your knees slightly bent but not locked. Take a position with your feet about eight inches apart and bend your knees so that the weight of your body is in balance between the heels and the balls of your feet. The rest of your body should be in a straight line with your arms hanging loosely at your side. Let your belly hang out. Don't force it out, but don't hold it in either. Belly breathe. Your back should be straight but not rigid and your pelvis should be relaxed. Hold this position for two minutes.

Aerobic Exercises

Aerobic exercises are those that increase heartbeat and oxygen intake. Active aerobic sports that involve running and jumping and bending help bring oxygen to your brain. John Reeves, director of sports and recreation at the University of Rochester, describes the advantages and disadvantages of many common aerobic exercises, most of which you can do indoors:[14]

Jump rope. This is a good and very inexpensive aerobic exercise. You can burn ten to twelve calories per minute at a fairly steady pace. You don't have to go outside and you can even do it in a hotel room. The disadvantage is that it is boring and, therefore, you probably wouldn't want to do it every day.

Racquetball, handball, and squash. Each sport burns about eight calories a minute and they are all good aerobic exercises. The advantage is that they are a lot of fun. The disadvantage is that special facilities and partners are needed to play these games.

Swimming. One of the best all-around exercises, it is especially good for cardiovascular fitness. Swimming is very easily regulated to your capacity. It burns around eight calories a minute. The only disadvantage is that you have to find a place to do it.

Tennis. A fine form of aerobic exercise, tennis is a good competitive activity and very enjoyable, but, again, you have to find a facility and a partner. It burns about six calories per minute.

Aerobic dance or exercise. Both burn from six to nine calories per minute. These social activities are good not only for the cardiovascular system but for flexibility. You may need a course with a leader and a group to spur you on. However, with programs on cable TV or on cassettes, and in books, it is possible to follow an aerobic dance or exercise program right in your own home.

Machines. Treadmills, rowing machines, and bicycles are fine methods of aerobic exercise. They burn about ten calories a minute. Such machines can be purchased starting at about 100 dollars.

Jogging will burn fourteen calories per minute and downhill skiing about ten calories per minute. A brisk walk, all experts agree, is one of the best all-around, safest exercises. It will burn about six calories a minute and not cost you anything. You can enjoy the environment and appreciate life. Many famous people have made decisions while walking—Harry Truman and John Steinbeck, for example.

Physical fitness experts believe it is wise to do aerobic exercises two days a week to keep your cardiovascular system in good shape and to perform anaerobic exercises (strengthening without increased oxygen intake), such as lifting free weights, three times a week to keep muscles toned and strong.

5

Music for the Mind

If a male canary is deafened in adulthood, the quality of its song deteriorates to the point where it becomes indistinguishable from that of a bird who was deafened as a juvenile—before it had ever sung. This suggests to researchers that brain pathways for song control remain plastic in adulthood and require continued access to auditory feedback to maintain a learned motor skill—singing.[1]

Singing, hearing, and making music are not just for bird brains. Music is being studied intensively today as a means of improving and maintaining brain and body functions. It has been shown to be beneficial for muscular development, physical coordination, a sense of timing, mental concentration, memory skills, visual and hearing development, and control of stress.

Music, therefore, is a readily available, highly effective tool that you can use today to improve both your cognitive and physical abilities.

The ancient Greeks knew that all along. They worshiped Apollo, god of healing and music, and believed each musical mode, rhythm, and instrument created its own special response. Modern medical practitioners are just finding out that the Greeks were right. In fact, there are now music therapists who use their skills to aid the disabled. And more and more therapists are helping the healthy improve function with music, since there is increasing evidence that this is not only possible but highly desirable: If you learn a musical instrument in adulthood, take up singing, or really concentrate on what the orchestra is playing (there is a difference between hearing and really listening), you can strengthen your body, organize your thinking, and improve your coordination.

The cerebellum is devoted to the regulation of the sort of movements we execute when playing musical instruments. Current research suggests that one of its fundamental functions may be to help us learn and remember new movements, such as playing the piano.[2] Further, it is suggested that the ability of the motor system to adapt to learning special movements may be significant in cases where damage to other parts of the brain requires reorganization. It makes sense, therefore, that exercising the cerebellum with music may modify nerve function in the healthy and compensate for impairment due to wear and tear as the years pass.

Frank Wilson, M.D., chief of neurology at Kaiser-Permanente Medical Center, Walnut Creek, and an assistant clinical professor of neurology at the University of California, San Francisco, points out that it takes more of the brain to control the small muscles of the body, which we use when we play a musical instrument, than to control the large muscles we use when we swing a tennis racket.[3]

Dr. Wilson himself began music lessons at the age of 40. "At first I felt clumsy, but then an amazing transformation seemed to take place," he says. "By the end of my sixth month, my hands were suddenly making music that I had been hearing in my head since the beginning."

He said he first became fascinated with how the human brain and body coordinate to produce music while watching his 11-year-old daughter play Chopin's Fantasy Impromptu on the piano: "It struck me that there was something wonderful going on. Learning to play the piano involves a wide range of human skills that we use in almost all our daily activities. I thought as a neurologist, I should know about this process. I wanted to know how the brain functions when a musician plays a fast passage on a musical instrument. We all have the ability to do it, but, of course, we are not all willing to make the effort to practice until we can do it."

What about talent? "First of all," says Dr. Wilson, "talent is not very well defined, and in some sense it is a destructive word. People use 'talent' to talk themselves or others out of playing an instrument. The key to success in music, as in sports, is having the right goals. If you set out to sound like a professional or try for the stage, your attitude is self-defeating."

He notes that if you consider yourself a beginner in music as you would if you were learning a new sport, you will succeed. He maintains that "musical performance demands the same type of training needed by athletes. The only difference from a physical point of view between musicians and athletes is that musicians are concerned with the smaller muscles of the body—especially those of the hands and perhaps the mouth—and they rely on their hearing more than their vision.

Dr. Wilson compares playing an instrument to jogging:

> Jogging has become popular because people aren't concerned with coming in first in a race as a measure of their success. They are compelled by the knowledge that they are extending themselves and enjoying the experience. If they run a mile or more than they did the last time, or run the same distance faster than before, they have succeeded. The same can be true of music. If the musicians are compelled by the knowledge that they are reaching new limits and sharing the experience with others—if in a band or group lessons—they are more likely to succeed. If you

play a difficult piece more smoothly than before or move on to something even more challenging, that should be your reward. You do feel wonderful when you have mastered something that's difficult. It gives you a terrific lift.

The "lift" you get from music, Dr. Wilson and other researchers agree, is as much physiological as it is psychological.

Did you ever consider why people prefer stereo to monaural music? According to researchers, it is because it stimulates more nerves in your brain. According to Dr. Manfred R. Schroeder, a physicist associated with AT&T Bell Laboratories in New Jersey, the more stimulation of the nerves, the greater the enjoyment.[4] He said that the nerve signals reaching the brain from the ears can work at cross purposes. If the signals are similar enough and if they arrive at nearly the same time, stimulation of the brain's nerves can actually be inhibited. Such may be the case with monaural music, which presents an almost identical sound in both ears. Since stereo, on the other hand, delivers different sounds to each ear, the auditory nerves send different messages to the brain. As a result, more brain nerves are excited.

One reason that music stimulates our nerves so effectively is that it has rhythm and tempo—and so do we. The continuous beat of our hearts is the most fundamental of all musical rhythms. Listen to the primitive drum, for example, and you'll hear a beating heart. It is the pulsing or flowing of the music in time, and not the melody, that compels us to move.

Tempo, on the other hand, refers to the rate of speed at which a piece of music is played. If rhythm makes us want to move, tempo affects how fast. It can pace our work and make it more fun. Just consider the popularity of jogging with earphones and of aerobic dancing.

The effect of music is evidently an inborn phenomenon. A number of experiments have shown that it stimulates movement in newborn and even in unborn babies.

Elaine Nichols, unit coordinator of Monmouth Medical Center, Long Branch, New Jersey, reported that Bach, Beethoven, and Brahms are used in the hospital nursery to stimulate newborn infants. Music by Vivaldi is also played because its violins and extremes of high and low pitch are better heard by babies. Nichols recommends that fathers sing to their unborn children because the father's deeper bass tones are better received through the amniotic fluid than the mother's higher tones.

In several centers in the United States and Israel, unborn babies are being stimulated by the application of headphones from portable cassette players to their mother's abdomen. Fetal breathing movements and body movements are now considered a good index of an unborn child's well-being. The influence on fetal well-being was examined in 20 women who listened to pop or classical music through earphones. An ultrasound scanner allowed direct observation of the fetus's body movements and breathing movements. The researchers found a significant decrease in breathing activity in fetuses while their mothers listened to their preferred type of music—whether it was rock or Beethoven made no difference. When music that the mother liked came through the headphones, it soothed the unborn infant.[5]

A study made by Milton Senn at Brown University showed that regular music stimulation programs for newborns produced IQ gains of 27 to 30 points over babies not in such programs.

Humans have long used the rhythm and tempo of music to make repetitive tasks easier, such as "toting that barge" and "lifting that bale." Three researchers at Stanford University set out to determine just how brain, muscle, and music work together to achieve greater ease of movement. Monica Grenier Safranek, Gail Koshland, and Gay Raymond first studied the electrical patterns emanated by flexion and extension of the elbow in women age 18 to 35 while performing a motor task without listening to rhythm. The subjects were asked to hit three targets in the following pattern: Target 1, one time; Target 2, three times; Target 3, two times. Each woman, the Stanford researchers reported, had her own personal rhythm. The subjects practiced the target hitting until they became skilled at it. The investigators point out that one assumption made about a skilled motor performance is that it reflects the most efficient recruitment of motor units (nerves and muscles that work together) because these units are activated more quickly and in greater synchronization than during unskilled performance.

When an even rhythm was played, the electrical signals recorded from the elbow muscles were decreased and created a more even pattern. When an uneven rhythm was played, the signals from the elbow muscles increased and were irregular, in a pattern similar to when a person is unskilled at a motor task. The researchers concluded that even rhythm aids efficiency in movement and produces action similar to that usually seen in skilled performance of motor tasks.[6]

Rhythm and tempo are not only useful in coordinating muscle action; they are also a means of altering mood.

A certified music therapist with a great interest in music therapy for the healthy, Shelly Katsch, M.A., C.M.T., of New York City, vice president of the National Association of Music Therapy, points out that music involves the right side of the brain, where emotions and feelings are located:

> Music communicates emotions—the very deep level of feeling that you sometimes can't express in

words. Furthermore, playing an instrument or working with music directly affects your sense of creativity and accomplishment. You can develop a stronger sense of self—of self-esteem. You can re-experience the joy of sound making. Many adults have lost the natural love for making sounds that children have because as youngsters they were told to "be quiet" when they made noise by vocalizing repetitive sounds. They became inhibited.[7]

Katsch and other musicologists say that when you hear the sounds that you produce with your voice or a musical instrument, just like the canary mentioned at the beginning of this chapter, it helps you relearn how to make joyful sounds.

In addition to the emotional lift that making music can give us, it can help improve our ability to think.

Donald Shetler, Ed.D., professor of music education at the University of Rochester's Eastman School of Music, explains why music can be intellectually stimulating:

> There is a difference between hearing and really listening to music. The listener is intellectually involved. When you really listen, you go beyond just appreciating the surface things. You identify, discriminate, classify, synthesize, detect formal and stylistic features in music. You make a conscious effort. When you perform, you are doing all those mind-expanding things the listener does, but you also add the physical functioning as well. You move your fingers and hands. Your muscles, joints, bones have to receive and exercise your commands. It is mental and physical skill. It demands concentration. There is an esthetic satisfaction and feedback that is self-renewing. Whether you just listen to or perform music, that feedback involves accomplishment, challenge and self-fulfillment. It is a peak experience.[8]

Think of a Song
Think of a song you know very well. Try reciting the words silently to yourself, without the melody in mind, and stop when you first stumble. Now try it with the melody—you should get further.

Dr. Jon Eisenson, a Stanford University Medical Center professor emeritus of hearing and speech science, uses music to treat patients unable to speak because of strokes or other brain injuries that affect the left side of the brain. Music and melody fall under the right hemisphere's jurisdiction, and Eisenson maintains that even the most severely impaired speechless (aphasic) person's recovery can be enhanced if the significant role of the brain's right hemisphere is recognized.[9]

Singing and speaking come from different areas of the brain. One has only to think of Mel Tillis, the popular country singer who stuttered terribly when he spoke but was able to sing his way up the music charts.

So singing is good for your brain. It makes words easier to remember and offers more efficient feedback than speaking. Alone, it stimulates a different area of the brain than speech and also provides an emotional release.

What if you can't carry a tune?

David Sudnow, a former sociology professor at New York University, who now teaches the piano to adults, maintains that anyone can carry a tune. "If you think you can't carry a tune," says Sudnow, "it is because someone inhibited you as a child and now you can't open your mouth and let the sound out." He maintains that he can teach anyone to carry a tune in a few sessions.[10]

According to Karl U. Smith, a retired University of Wisconsin psychology professor, you need only look in the mirror to see if you have real musical talent. He maintains that "left-faced people are better singers." He studied facedness for many years and says that Frank

Sinatra, opera singers, and famous composers all are "left-faced."

You can tell your facedness, Smith maintains, by looking in the mirror and seeing which eyebrow is higher, which eye is more open, and on which side your smile is more pronounced. Muscular control of the face, he explains, is divided. The right side controls the consonant-forming lips and tongue, while the left side steers the vowel-shaping cheeks and throat. Stronger vowel makers make better singers, he continues. His theory is that you can't develop acute perception of tone without being able to produce tones to some degree.[11]

So you're right-faced and can't be a great singer, but can you play the piano?

The professor-turned-music teacher, David Sudnow, has been very successful in using electronic piano keyboards and videotapes to teach adults to play music "by ear" in four to eight weeks. He says that your hands can learn to play a musical instrument just as your feet can learn to dance. It becomes automatic.

He compares improvised music-making—playing by ear without notes—to ordinary talking. In the former, there is an instrument lying outside the body; in the latter, all of the parts being used are body parts. Yet a true incorporation does occur and it makes sense to speak of the instrument as a genuine extension of the body, just as it makes sense to say that the blind person comes to feel the pavement or the wall through the tip of his or her cane.

Many physical effects can be derived from using your body to make music. In fact, merely listening to music has been found to lower blood pressure and to affect galvanic skin resistance and respiratory rates. It has also been shown to affect the pattern of electrical activity of the muscles and nerves, and thus its physiological effects on function have been measured.[12]

What other physical fitness benefits can you achieve with a musical instrument?

Rochester's Dr. Shetler points out that playing woodwinds improves breath control and increases oxygen to the brain. (Check with your physician if you suffer from high blood pressure before taking up a woodwind.)

The piano and violin are excellent for finger manipulation and can improve your hand-eye coordination. And, he maintains:

> Singing is one of the best therapeutic measures for both mind and body. It gives you the opportunity to extend vocal sounds. Ordinary speech does not extend sound, but a long note does. Thus, singing exercises the larynx and vocal cords and feeds back to the area of the brain that receives music and voice sounds. Exercising any muscle strengthens it and, of course, the breathing apparatus is made of muscle. Further, singing is fun, particularly if you sing familiar songs and tape them on a recorder. You can enjoy listening to yourself.[13]

Music can eliminate loneliness and solitude, which can interfere with cognition. It is the only art in which you can be both the doer and the audience. You can perform just for yourself and you aren't dependent upon others for feedback.

How much will you have to practice to improve the physiology of your brain?

Neurologist Frank Wilson, M.D., says that most of the physical and intellectual benefits of music are derived from practicing. Before he leaves for the office each day he practices for an hour. Most experts agree that an hour a day is best. Some say you can break it up into 15-minute segments. Others say it takes at least 15 minutes to warm up and 15 minutes to begin to derive benefits from the practice. In any event, Dr. Wilson recommends patience because it will take six months to a year before you really reap the full benefits of learning to play an instrument in adulthood.[14]

Choosing a Teacher
You can learn by yourself, but a good teacher can help you progress. Make sure the instructor's personality meshes with yours. Many are used to teaching children and not adults. The old European Conservatory type of teaching with lots of scales and exercises is passé; playing songs right from the beginning is the preferred method today. It's more enjoyable.

Good sources of information about teachers are friends who are already taking lessons; local music stores; school music instructors; and Ys or other community centers. Group instruction is widely available and allows you to share your experience and make new friends.

Selecting an Instrument
The piano, most experts agree, is probably easiest for an adult because you don't have to learn to make a tone on it as you do with wind instruments or violins. Piano keyboards have become computerized and portable, just like guitars, so you can carry them with you. There are many second-hand instruments around, so before you lay out a great deal of money, borrow one or buy a second-hand one to see if you really wish to continue with your lessons.

The following is an evaluation of the degree of difficulty of various instruments provided by the American Music Conference, the national group made up of instrument producers and others interested in promoting the playing of musical instruments.

Easiest: autoharp, electric keyboard, bongo drums, recorder, chord organ, ukulele, conga drums.

Fairly easy: accordion, drum set, acoustic guitar, electric guitar, banjo, harmonica, concertina, mandolin.

Average: also saxophone, flute, tenor sax, baritone sax, organ, trombone, clarinet, piano (upright), tuba, cornet/trumpet, sousaphone, xylophone.

Fairly difficult: bass viol, cello, French horn, viola, violin.

Most difficult: bassoon, harp, English horn, oboe.

6

Memories Are Made of . . .

Are you as intelligent as you once were?

Would you like to be more intelligent than you have ever been?

Intelligence is the capacity to learn. *Learning* is based on the acquisition of new knowledge about the environment. *Memory* is its retention.

Research psychologists and neurobiologists have just recently been able to actually see the changes that occur in the chemistry and electrical output of the brain cells as learning takes place and memories are stored.

What had been only surmised in the past can now be proven. By learning new things and by using your intellectual capabilities more efficiently, you can actually change the physical properties of your brain. These changes can take place no matter what your age!

As we have noted before, people do not use the full capacity of their brains. Some use more than others. There are geniuses among us and "sloths." We all use our brains better on some days than others. You know, for example, that when you are harassed and tired, you may not be able to remember your own phone number or where you put your car keys. The information is stored in your memory, but you can't recall it. Your learning ability may not be impaired, but your ability to perform is temporarily reduced.

We discussed in earlier chapters how information is fed into your brain through your senses. If you need glasses and don't wear them, your brain is not going to be able to perceive written directions and learn a new way to put something together. If the environment is so noisy that you can't hear your lover say, "I love you," you won't be able to recall that tender moment. Your sense perceptions have to be keen and your state of alertness, your emotions, motivations, and environmental situation have to all be conducive to learning and retention if beneficial changes in your brain cells are to occur.

Neurobiologists are using powerful microscopes to *see* and minute electrodes to *hear* those changes in a single brain cell as learning takes place.

They can see that when a cat learns or when its brain is stimulated electrically, its brain forms new connections between neurons by the branching out of their dendrites, the spiderlike "sensors" emanating from the shaft of a nerve. Similar nerve growth has been observed in hamsters and rats. These results are interpreted to mean that nerve cells show changes in their form and function as they take part in increased "internal traffic."

Marian Cleeves Diamond, Ph.D., and James Connor, Ph.D., of the Department of Physiology and Anatomy at the University of California at Berkeley, reported in 1980 that they were able, for the first time, to show that there can be an actual increase in the dendrites in the cortex of the aged brain.[1]

Changes have also been measured in the synapses, the gaps between nerve cells where information is exchanged and the nerve cell is either fired into action or blocked from reacting. The learning results not only in adding or subtracting synapses but in altering the strength of such contacts.

Without memory there can, of course, be no learning or high intelligence. But how do the changes in a single cell work together to produce a memory? How and where are memories stored?

Try to go back as far as you can in your memory. Whatever it was you remembered was in your head for almost as many years as you've been alive. You have just used your long-term memory.

Now, pick up a phone book and select any number. Close the book and write it down. Wait one minute and, without looking at the number again, try to write it down. Did you forget? The phone number probably remained with you just long enough for you to write it down the first time. In this case, you have used your short-term memory.

Your short-term memory can hold between five and ten pieces of information. Unless you repeat to yourself what you are trying to remember, the data is typically forgotten in less than a minute. Your temporary storage system is used, for example, when you recall what someone said a moment ago. Your small-capacity "working memory" plays a critical role in your reasoning and comprehension.

In contrast, the capacity of your long-term memory is vast. It normally contains records of enormous numbers of facts and experiences. You can preserve information for many years without making any conscious effort at all to retain it.

In the mid-1970s, researchers at Bell Laboratories in Murray Hill, New Jersey, studied both short-term and long-term memory.

To test short-term memory, Max V. Mathews, Sc.D., David E. Meyer, Ph.D., now of the University of Michigan, and Saul Sternberg, Ph.D., gave subjects a set of numbers to learn and then asked them if certain digits were in that list. They measured the time it took a person to answer.

Based on the speed with which the group in general replied, the Bell researchers concluded that our minds can search through a memorized list at least three times faster than our eyes can. We are capable of making a mental search at the rate of 25 to 30 digits per second.

Long-term memory, the Bell researchers believe, is arranged like a thesaurus: Words with related meanings seem to be stored "near" one another in the brain. Nearness, however, may correspond to either physical proximity or richness of nerve connections. They base their belief on the fact that we can recognize and pronounce a printed word faster if it is related in meaning to an immediately preceding word—such as *doctor* to *nurse*—than if it is unrelated—like *doctor* and *vase*.

One logical explanation of why long-term memory is probably stored this way, they said, is that retrieving a word from long-term memory temporarily increases nerve activity in the locations of other nearby words. This "overflow" activation reduces the process needed to recognize a related word, and thus speeds up reaction time.[2]

Now, you can see why "association," a technique used in mnemonics, is so effective (see pages 95–97).

Speed is essential when using long-term memory. The search rate of 30 items per second estimated for short-term memory would be much too slow for finding a particular word among the thousands stored in the archives of your brain's long-term memory. Reading, writing, or speaking a single sentence would take several minutes if we had to rely on this recall time. The speed of searching our long-term memory is measured in milliseconds. We can, for example, recognize the meaning of more than 100,000 words in less than a second.

But how does short-term memory become long-term?

No one knows for certain, but there are clues. It is well known that a person who suffers a concussion can't remember what happened immediately before the accident, so-called retrograde amnesia. A patient receiving electroshock for depression also suffers from memory problems. The jolting of the brain in both cases somehow short-circuits the processing of short-term memory into long-term.

We must be able to file what we experience for future use or we couldn't function in the world. One of the greatest quests today in psychology and neuroscience is to find how and where memory is stored in the brain.

It is known that the storage of data in our brains requires three basic things:

① *Registration.* Our brain must receive the information from our senses.
② *Consolidation.* The information has to be stored either short-term or long-term.
③ *Retrieval.* We have to be able to call up that information when we want it.

The first major breakthrough in the scientific understanding of memory occurred in 1936 when Canadian neurosurgeon Wilder Penfield, M.D., touched an electric needle to the surface of the brain of a patient who was awake, and that patient began recalling an event as vividly as if it were happening right then and there. Dr. Penfield's experiment has been repeated by others, but no one has yet identified the exact location in the brain of the memory bank or banks.[3]

There are hints based on work with people whose memories have been affected by injury or disease. It has been determined, for example, that damage to a portion of the side of the brain, the medial temporal cortex, does not interfere greatly with a person's ability to learn, but that person forgets whatever he has learned almost immediately. He can't change short-term memory into long-term. Damage to another part of the bottom of the brain, the diencephalon, which contains the control centers for the endocrine glands and the basic drives, limits the ability to form new memories but leaves almost intact the ability to retain what was previously learned. In certain cases of tumors and intractable epilepsy, half the brain may be removed and yet the memories stored and the ability to record new ones may remain intact.

Today, research on memory is primarily physiological. Scientists now believe that memories are stored electrochemically. This belief is based on the second big breakthrough in the study of memory, which occurred in the 1970s. That's when neurotransmitters were discovered. They are chemicals, secreted by the brain's nerve cells, that carry messages to other nerve cells. They hold the key to the acquisition, consolidation, and retrieval of memories.

Before the discovery of neurotransmitters, doctors maintained that memory deficits were caused by "hardening of the arteries." That belief has all but been abandoned today and scientists are now concentrating on the problems caused by the failure of brain cells to "converse" with each other.

Remember that old belief that fish is brain food? There may be some truth to it because fish contains high levels of choline, as do meat and eggs. Choline is taken from food in the digestive tract by the blood and carried to the brain, where it is turned into acetylcholine, a neurotransmitter that aids in sending messages from cell to cell. Although acetylcholine is quantitatively a relatively minor neurotransmitter in the central nervous system, it has a prime role in intellectual activity, including memory. The transmitter is found in highest concentration in the cerebral cortex, the caudate nucleus, and in parts of the limbic system where the choline-secreting nerves are located.

In the aged, the capability of transferring information from one cell to another or to a target organ is markedly reduced. This is due in part to the amount of acetylcholine

in the cell and in part to the ability to use what is there.[4]
An enzyme called cholinesterase is believed to be largely
responsible for the destruction of acetylcholine, and there
is work going on to find drugs that will either block the
enzyme or increase the cell's output of acetylcholine. As
you will see in Chapter 9, efforts are also being made to
increase the amount of lecithin, which contains choline,
and choline itself in the diet. It has also been reported that
the production of acetylcholine is impaired by reduction
in the respiratory rate (see Brain Breathing exercises,
pages 70–73).

There is no doubt that in time drugs will be developed
that will enhance memory, but what can you do about it
naturally?

Since our long-term memory is stored quite efficiently,
what we want to improve is our short-term memory and
our retrieval of long-term memory. These are the problems about which many people begin to complain after
the age of 35. In fact, it is so common that researchers call
it "benign senile forgetfulness."

We all have experienced meeting someone and being
unable to remember that person's name. *Nominal memory*, which seems to give many people over 30 some difficulty at times, involves being able to recall what someone
or something is called.

We all have also experienced forgetting where we put
something, such as our glasses or a paper. While "losing"
something can happen at any age, it does become a more
common phenomenon in those over 30. *Spatial memory*
involves knowing where an object belongs, including ourselves. When was the last time you stood before the refrig-
erator or a filing cabinet and said, "Now, why did I come
here?"

You may suddenly recall a person's name or remember
where you put your keys or why you entered a room. Why

did you have difficulty remembering? How were you able to eventually recall the name or the place you were seeking?

Psychologists have long been aware that emotions play a significant role in the memory process. Sigmund Freud found that during therapy patients were able to recall incidents that had long been forgotten. He reasoned that certain events had been forgotten because they were upsetting to the patient. He called this process of "motivated forgetting" repression.

A similar process occurs in amnesia. After undergoing a particularly traumatic event, such as a criminal assault, a person may have no memory of the entire episode, or some of the details may be lost to him. According to current theory, amnesia sometimes occurs when people are unable to face the reality of their own behavior or the situation in which they find themselves.

An interesting phenomenon of memory retrieval is illustrated in the film *City Lights*. Charlie Chaplin saves a drunken millionaire from suicide and becomes his friend. The millionaire, when sober, forgets who Charlie is and has him thrown out. Drunk again, the millionaire embraces Charlie as his friend. Scientific experiments have confirmed this process. Subjects given alcohol and made drunk were asked to hide a set of keys. Unable to retrieve the keys when sober, they were made drunk again and then could easily locate the lost objects.

Exactly how we remember and why we forget is still not clear to scientists, although it is known that physical and emotional factors affect our memories. Depressed people frequently complain of poor memory—especially short-term memory. Older people, as well, sometimes find it difficult to recall current experiences, but can remember events that took place fifty years ago. Despite the fact that there is still much to be learned about memory, you can increase your ability to turn short-term memories into long-term. It takes motivation and practice.

Memory training can produce spectacular results. In a report in *Science* in 1980, for example, researchers at Carnegie-Mellon University in Pittsburgh described how an undergraduate student with an average memory and average intelligence engaged in memory training for about one hour a day, three to five days a week, for more than a year and a half. He was able to increase the amount of information that his short-term memory held from 7 to 79 digits. Furthermore, his ability to remember digits after the session—his long-term memory—also improved. In the beginning he could recall virtually nothing after an hour's session; after 20 months of practice, he could recall more than 80 percent.[5]

The system used at Carnegie-Mellon was actually first reported in 477 B.C. and is widely used to improve the memories of stroke victims. It is called *mnemonics*—the principle of associating unknown material with something familiar; the advantage is that it relieves the burden on short-term memory because recall can be achieved through a single association with an already existing item stored in long-term memory.

The trick is to make the association between what we want to remember and what we have already remembered vivid.

Association Practice

Associations are the links that hold the intellect together. The following is an exercise that will help you make associations. Try to find the word that fits with each of the other four words. For example, what word would you attach to:

SET   BURN   LIGHT   BEAM   _____

If you associated "sun" with them, you'd have had the answer. But it is the practice of associating that counts, not the right answers. When you have spare time waiting for an appointment or are sitting at a boring meeting, try to make up your own lists. Here are ten more examples.

1. LESS DEAD UP REAR _____
2. WAY TIDE BACK WHITE _____
3. ORDER MAN BOX AIR _____
4. LIGHT TO ONE SOME _____
5. LIGHT STOUT GOOD BIG _____
6. WEATHER STOCK CARD NEWS _____
7. EXAMINE WORD DOUBLE ROAD _____
8. HAT CHAIR LIGHT FLYING _____
9. AT SKI ROPE HIGH _____
10. LACE TIE BREAK LINE _____

Answers

10. NECK	5. HEARTED
9. JUMP	4. DAY
8. HIGH	3. MAIL
7. CROSS	2. WATER
6. REPORT	1. END

The more concrete the item to be recalled, the more unusual or ridiculous the image created to associate it with, the easier it will be to remember.

Suppose you want to remember a shopping list of bread, eggs, flour, and orange juice. The first thing you might do is picture a loaf of bread breaking open and an egg falling out. Then picture a pitcher of orange juice being poured into a hole in a flour bag. Each item is linked to the subsequent one via the ridiculous image. By using mnemonics, stroke patients who couldn't remember the days and the months of the year were soon able to master the whole list of U.S. Presidents.

Another ancient trick is to think of a room and picture putting each thing you want to remember on some object in the room. Suppose you wish to remember to pick up the clothes at the cleaners, take a letter to the post office, and stop for some bread. Picture your living room with clothes on the armchair, a letter on the coffee table, and bread on the sofa. The same would work for a long number. Suppose you want to remember 143054. You could picture 14 on the chair, 30 on the coffee table, and 54 on the sofa. Then you can easily remember the number 143054 when you picture walking into that room.

What else can you do?

Stay in good health. People with poor circulation, collagen disease, or other physical problems suffer more of a mental decline than those who are in reasonably good health. Successful treatment of physical ailments may improve your memory.

Check your diet and medications. A number of drugs in common use, such as those for ulcers, anxiety, or high blood pressure, may affect one's ability to remember. A diet that is not sufficiently nutritious (see Chapter 9) can also affect the ability to remember. If you suspect either your medications or your diet, check with your physician. Sometimes merely a change in medication or prescribed dietary supplements may improve memory significantly.

Pay attention. One problem identified with people who have difficulty learning is that it is often not their memory at fault, so much as their concentration. There is a decline in the ability to discriminate and retain after 15 to 45 minutes of studying at any age. Therefore, you should take five- to ten-minute breaks. An intermission gives the brain a chance to *consolidate* and *organize* what has just been run through it.

Say it out loud. When trying to remember something —especially short-term—say it out loud. Hearing something helps you retain it. Noise can interfere with your retaining something short-term, so try to keep your environment quiet when you are learning something new.

Use categories. Researchers believe that related memories may be stored next to each other. You can name the states in the Union more easily, for example, if you use geographical divisions rather than a random method. Grocery lists can be remembered easily if you use product categories, such as "dairy," "meats," "canned goods."

Use cadence. If you set what you are trying to remember to music or make it into a rhyme, you will remember it more easily.

Break things into chunks. The nine-digit zip code proposed by the postal service was two numbers too long for most people's short-term memory. Therefore, if you have to remember a long number, break it into chunks. A number such as 555619101 can more easily be remembered as 555 619 101.

Review. According to current research, when you review, you strengthen the connections and associations between the nerve cells in your brain, but it does little good to repeat and repeat in rapid succession what you are trying to memorize. Since initial consolidation of information from short-term to long-term is thought to occur within ten minutes of the event, the first review should take place ten minutes after you've completed your study. Further reviews should be done one day, one week, one month, and then six months after the study to make maximum use of consolidation.

Memorize something each day. The more you use your brain to retain information, the more you will be able to do it efficiently. The more you remember, the more you can remember.

Intend to remember. Psychiatrist William James wrote: "What we are interested in is what sticks in our consciousness. Everything else we get rid of as quickly as possible."

Always repeat instructions. When given instructions or directions, repeat aloud what has been said or written. This will help clarify the steps in your mind and you will be able to remember them better. One of the theories about why this works well is that the right half of the brain is used for visual memory and the left half for verbal memory. By looking at instructions and then repeating aloud, the whole brain is employed to remember.

Organize, organize, organize. This is one of the most important memory aids. Many middle-aged and older people who made an effort to put things in proper order when younger become careless once they find there are less demands on their time. Before beginning the day or a project, think through the sequence you will follow. Do things in order of priority, naturally, but if you have a task that is tedious, try to do that first. You'll be less likely to forget projects that are more interesting.

Make associations in order to remember names. One often-tried method of remembering a person's name when introduced is to make a picture association with the name. Mrs. White could be associated with a white duck, for example. Repeating the name after someone gives it to you also helps, as does asking the person the origin of the name, if that is appropriate. You can also rhyme the name in your mind: "Jones" with "bones," for example. Try anything that works to "fix" the person's name in your memory.

Use your common senses. Some of us remember what we have seen better than what we have heard. And others remember what they have heard better than what they have seen. Which one are you? Remember the house where you grew up? Can you picture it clearly . . . the furniture, the yard, the kitchen? Can you remember the discussions at the dinner table or hear your mother giving you advice as you left for school? If you can picture the house better than you can remember the sounds there, you are more visual than verbal.

What about your smell memory? Actually, many scientists maintain that smell is everyone's best memory. Once you have identified a smell, you never forget it. In any case, it is through our senses that we gather information. We can use all of them to help us remember.

When you are trying to memorize something, be conscious of how it smells, sounds, and looks. Try this experiment to prove how "sensing" can help you remember. Take a bottle of toilet water or a bar of sweet-smelling soap. Sniff it and read a paragraph and note the meaning of the paragraph. Sniff the perfumed object again. Tomorrow, take the perfumed object and sniff it again. You should recall the paragraph immediately.

The following are two further tests of your memory. You can judge for yourself how much you need to improve it.

List Memorization
Look at this list of words for five seconds and then on a
blank piece of paper write as many as you can remember.

DOG	STONE
CAT	WINTER
BIRD	WHITE
SHOVEL	WILL
SKILL	WENT
HOUSE	TEN
ROBIN	LIFE
GRANT	LATE
HORSE	STAR
CRAG	STAIR
ELIZABETH TAYLOR	HONOR

How many did you write down? Probably no more than
ten but, undoubtedly, you remembered Elizabeth Taylor.
If you could have established associations as readily with
the other words, you would have had a perfect score.

Face Identification
Look at the pictures on page 103 and the first names
under them for 12 seconds. Then turn the page, look at
the pictures again, and try to write down the names on a
piece of paper. Again, if you had practiced association—
"hooking" what is to be remembered with something already filed—you would have gotten a perfect score.

Further Memorization Exercises

    If, in my retirement to the humble station of a pri-
vate citizen, I am accompanied with the esteem and
approbation of my fellow citizens, trophies obtained
by the blood-stained steel or the tattered flags of the
tented field, will never be envied. The care of human

life and happiness, and not their destruction, is the
first and only legitimate object of good government.
—Thomas Jefferson, March 31, 1809

Write a headline that describes the meaning of the
above paragraph.

Underline the important words.

Sing the words in the entire paragraph. Then read
them aloud.

Now close the book and write down as much of the
paragraph as you can remember.

How did you do?

Now, memorize the following poem:

Some weigh their pleasure by their lust,
Their wisdom by their rage of will:
Their treasure is their only trust;
A cloaked craft their store of skill.
But all the pleasure that I find
Is to maintain a quiet mind.

My wealth is health and perfect ease;
My conscience clear by chief defense;
I neither seek by bribes to please,
Nor by deceit to breed offense.
Thus do I live; thus will I die;
Would all did so as well as I!
—From *"My Mind to Me a Kingdom"*
Sir Edward Dyer

Which memorization exercise was easier? Singing lines,
underlining, and rhyming all help you remember because
they form "connections." Poetry and music exercise the
right side of your brain.

Photos by Grant Winter

Tony

Joan

Gina

Peter

Barbara

Mary Ann

Lily

Marjorie

John

Photos by Grant Winter

Put Away Your Calculator

A good exercise for the left side of your brain is to add, multiply, and subtract without the aid of a calculator. If you don't keep refreshing your memory with the answers to mathematical manipulations, you will have increasing difficulty retrieving the answers to numerical problems. To help yourself keep the machinery oiled, count up to 60 by threes, starting with the number two. Count back from 100 by sixes.

Whenever you are waiting in line or you can't sleep, try your own version of this number exercise.

7

Increase Your Ability to Learn

Learning usually involves two facets:
①• The accumulation of information and the efficient storage of that information in our brains, as discussed in the previous chapter.
②• The use of that information in response to some stimulus.

Your chronological age is really no excuse if your intellectual performance is not up to par.

The idea that great regressive changes in cognition can be expected as part of the normal aging process is no longer considered valid. In fact, some people not only show no deficit as the years go by, they actually increase in intellect.

Psychologists in the 1930s said that intelligence peaks in the late teens. In the 1940s they said intelligence peaks at age 25. In the 1950s, psychologists said the peak was in the thirties. Now psychologists are telling us that one type of intelligence peaks in the forties while another peaks between the ages of 60 and 70.

How can age and intelligence be truly evaluated in humans?

There are two basic techniques:

Cross-sectional. You take a group of people in different

decades—the twenties, forties, and fifties, for example —and compare how they do on tests.

Longitudinal. You begin studying people in their teens and test them periodically as they age.

The classic study was conducted by K. Warner Schaie, formerly director of the Gerontology Research Institute at the University of Southern California in Los Angeles, and now at Penn State University. During the course of a 21-year study of intellectual performance in aging adults, Schaie and his colleagues examined several thousand healthy volunteers ranging in age from 22 to 81. Subjects were called back at seven-year intervals for retesting. The most positive and provocative finding of this work is that at all ages the majority of people maintained their levels of intellectual competence—or actually improved—as they grew older. Even between the ages of 74 and 81, almost 10 percent of the people tested performed better than they had at younger ages.[1]

There are, however, basic problems with both cross-sectional and longitudinal studies. Max Fogel, Ph.D., supervising psychologist of Mensa, the organization of people who score in the 98th percentile on IQ tests, explains why: "First of all, young people today have a better education. Then there is the motivational factor. Younger people are more eager to do well on tests. They are more interested in impressing others and they are more socially active."[2] On the other hand, he explains, since longitudinal studies are done over a period of years, the selection factor interferes with results. People die as they get older. Therefore, you test survivors, a healthier and healthier population.

Despite the problems with testing, there is enough evidence from Dr. Schaie's study and many others to draw some general conclusions about the effects of age on intelligence.

First of all, Raymond B. Cattell and John Horn developed a theory in the 1960s that there are two basic types of intelligence, fluid and crystallized.[3]

① *Fluid intelligence,* also called performance intelligence, involves skills such as the coordination of your hands and reacting to a situation where speed is important. It requires quick judgment and is essentially nonverbal. Although this type of intelligence depends partly on education and experience, it is relatively independent of them and is thought to be most directly related to the functioning of the nervous system.

② *Crystallized intelligence,* also called verbal intelligence, involves the ability to use habits of judgment based on experience in order to solve problems. These habits have been crystallized—that is, they have taken a definite form—as a result of earlier learning. Crystallized intelligence includes an awareness of terms and concepts reflected in tests of general information and a knowledge of specific fields such as science and mathematics. Although strongly related to educational level and environment, this type of intelligence is in part dependent on fluid intelligence. It doesn't involve speed and tends to hold up very well as we age.

It is with fluid or performance intelligence that problems may arise as one gets older, since there is a slowing of messages between nerve cells, which results in slower reaction time. How much of a deficit occurs varies greatly. While a decline in intelligence may include more and more people as time goes by, it does not include everyone! For example, out of a hundred people in their forties, 20 may show an intellectual decline. In their fifties, an additional 30 persons may show a decline, and so on. But there are some who never do manifest a lessening of intellect.[4]

Why? There is no doubt that heredity and health have a lot to do with it, but so does continued intellectual exercise. Recently a number of researchers working with animals have shown that learning actually increases the strength of nerve transmission and changes the physical properties of nerve endings.[5-7] They are quite certain that the same holds true for humans and that much of the deficit attributed to aging is actually due to the lack of stimulation of those nerves involved in learning. It is known, from studies conducted at the NIA's Baltimore Gerontology Research Center, that continued intellectual pursuits preserve and even enhance functions in the elderly.

Teaching an old dog new tricks, therefore, aids mental functioning. It also prolongs life. A study of subjects over a 12-year period correlated maintenance of intellectual vigor with capacity to survive. Furthermore, aging business executives whose work requires sharp intellect show little or no weakening of their nervous systems compared with aging production workers.[8]

The inverse is also true. Remove stimulation and motivation and you dull cognition and may actually shorten your life.

What can you do to improve your learning, memory, and cognition?

First of all, you can consider the relationship between concentration, attention, alertness, memory, and organization. Concentration, by definition, means to bring one's efforts, faculties, to bear on one thing. When you pay attention, you are observant or watchful. When you are alert, you are vigilant and ready for action. And when you organize, you arrange things in a systematic manner. You use all of the above to record and recall memories.

While there is much yet to learn about memory storage and retrieval, the following exercises have proven through the years to strengthen that wonderful system we use to remember and recall.

Practice Your Powers of Observation
How much do you see without perceiving? There are many things common to our daily life that we do not really register in our minds or, if we do, we cannot recall. Just think of the varied stories eyewitnesses give when asked to describe the scene of an accident. The following test exercises your powers of observation:

1. On a caduceus, the staff carried by the god Hermes, which is used as an emblem of the medical profession, how many snakes are there below the wings?
2. On a flat map of the world, which continent is to the left of South America and which is to the right?
3. Whose picture is on a ten-dollar bill and what building is on the back?
4. Is the green light on top or bottom on the traffic light?
5. Which stripe is on top of the American flag, the red or white?
6. The Italian flag's colors are green, red, and white. In which order are they from left to right?
7. On which side does a bride stand at the altar?
8. What are the top and bottom numbers on a fever thermometer?
9. How many nails are on a dog's paw?
10. How many points are there on the maple leaf Canada uses on its flag?

Answers

1. Two snakes are wound around the staff.
2. Australia is on the left and Africa is on the right.
3. Alexander Hamilton and The Treasury Building.
4. The bottom.
5. Red.
6. Green, white, and red.
7. The right.

8. 92 and 6.
9. Five.
10. 11.

To continue to exercise your powers of observation, observe common things in your environment and make up your own quizzes for your family, friends, and/or co-workers. It's fun and will increase your ability to gather information from the world around you.

Attention Getter
There can be no learning without attention. Those who work in cognitive rehabilitation have found that it is not just memory that is a problem but also getting patients to pay attention. The centers are using computers with dots that flash on the screen as an exercise. You can use the traditional child's game of slap-the-hand. You place your hand on a table and your partner randomly tries to tap it before you withdraw it. Your partner should make the attempts irregularly so that you will not know when the tap is coming. This will help not only your attention but your reflexes.

Picking Out Priorities
Take a newspaper or magazine article, cover the headline, and read the article. Write your own headline and then summarize in one paragraph the most important material in the article. You should do this for at least one article every time you read a magazine or newspaper. It is really one of the best cognition exercises available because it helps you identify and organize important material.

Increase Your Arousal Level
Ask yourself, How important is it? Lee Iacocca, the man who saved the Chrysler car company, says that if it is

important, you will remember it. If you are trying to learn something or remember to do something, you first have to convince yourself of its importance. Why do you really want to remember or learn? It is like driving in a car and trying to remember your directions to a certain place. You'll find that the driver who must concentrate on the car and road will remember better than the passenger in the front seat.

You can also increase your arousal by proper breathing and exercise (see Chapter 4).

Use Your Sensory Strengths
If you find you are better at processing information by listening to it, use a tape recorder and read what you want to remember or do into the tape. Then play it back. If you are visually oriented, read and underline or use diagrams and sketching to consolidate information.

Don't Let Emotions Interfere
If something is on your mind, write down what is bothering you. This almost magically allows you to concentrate. Also see the relaxation exercises in Chapter 10.

Take Notes From Print or From Discussion
Taking down the salient points made by a TV talk-show guest is an excellent exercise. It encourages you to pay attention to what is important. Writing down the information from TV or your reading reenforces it in your memory and exercises your concentration and prioritizing.

Organize Your Information
Underline important pieces of information. Make lists. Take notes. Outline. Make questions up about what you are trying to learn. Identify supportive details. Circle the most important words that signal what you wish to learn or remember.

Set a List of Weekly and Daily Goals
Give the time and date you wish the goals to be attained.

Rehearse, Rehearse, Rehearse
As was discussed earlier, repetition creates changes in brain cells. If you want to learn something or perform better, keep rehearsing.

Keep a Diary
By recording what has happened during the day, you are evaluating what occurred. Reminiscing on paper has been found to be an excellent way of exercising mental functions. It is also a good emotional outlet.

Learn a New Language
There are many opportunities to learn a foreign language today, no matter what your age or where you live. There are adult schools, colleges, cassettes, computer programs, and cable TV courses.

Why should you make the effort?

Learning a new language is one of the best brain builders available. Although just how language processing is done by your brain is still being debated among neurolinguists, neurologists, psycholinguists, and a host of other specialists, all agree that it is a marvelous and complicated phenomenon.

For more than a hundred years, it was believed that language function was located in the left hemisphere, particularly in two key sections of the left front part of the cortex known as Broca's and Wernicke's areas, named respectively after two 19th-century neurologists. They discovered that lesions to these areas caused distinct types of inability to communicate. In Broca's aphasia, associated with lesions in the back of the frontal lobe of the left hemisphere near the area that controls speech, both speech and writing are usually severely affected. The difficulty in speaking is demonstrated by trouble finding a word or certain sounds. Nevertheless, the words are usually employed correctly and what is said often makes sense. In Wernicke's aphasia, associated with lesions farther back in the brain near the primary sound-receiving area in the left hemisphere, speech frequently is very fluent but meaningless.

Since the observations of Broca and Wernicke, others have found that producing good communication involves many parts of the brain. It is now believed that while various areas may specialize in certain aspects of language, there is a complicated, widespread interchange that occurs between the left and right hemispheres, the motor cortex, and even the deeper structures, including those involved with emotions.[9]

Therefore, by learning a new language, you will be greatly stimulating wide areas of your brain and exercising your memory, speech, and writing centers and generally benefiting your cognitive abilities.

Turn Off the TV and Read, Read
It is very easy to come home after a tiring day and turn on the TV, but greater benefits to your brain will accrue from reading—newspapers, magazines, or books. Reading requires more concentration, and what you are concentrating upon will usually be more nourishing to your brain. Youngsters often try to concentrate on their homework while watching TV. As they soon learn when they see their grades, concentration means focusing on one thing at a time.

Computers Are Good for Your Brain
Learning to use computers is excellent for your brain. You have to coordinate hand and eye, follow directions, and react quickly. Computer games are being used in most cognitive rehabilitation centers for those very reasons.

Computers have come down in price so that they are within the means of most households. By learning to use a computer, you will not only exercise your brain, you will receive a psychological lift because you have joined the Computer Age. There are also a lot of computerized learning programs available. Unlike human teachers, computers have infinite patience and can be available whenever you need them.

Play Games
The game is a basic phenomenon that provides challenge, interest, and fun. As mentioned above, video games are very useful, especially those requiring answers to questions or instant reactions to hit a target. Bridge and chess are excellent games to pursue because they require memory and judgment. Crossword puzzles and jigsaw puzzles are also excellent, the former for word recall and the latter for spatial judgments.

Set New Challenges
• Figure out what you really want and then develop the skills to get it!
• Make a list of your objectives for the next year and for the next five years. Study the list and then write down how you believe you can meet those aims. The next chapter will help you with the methods.

8

Mining Your Creativity

Creativity is not limited to painting, writing a novel, or to scientific innovations. It involves your ability to use your brain to change, renew, and recombine aspects of your life. Creativity means sensing the world with vigor and making new use of what you have perceived.

Children are naturally creative because everything is novel to them. Unfortunately, our school systems follow predetermined paths, and those who want to make new trails run into many boobytraps.

Creativity is not encouraged in adults either. Our youth-oriented society rarely considers the possibility that people past 65 years or even 80 years can produce creative solutions or products. True creativity, however, is not constrained by age nor does it require high intelligence or good grades. On the contrary, high IQ may inhibit the inner resources of the individual because of rigid self-criticism or rapid learning of cultural standards. The great ability to deduce according to the laws of logic and mathematics makes for disciplined thinkers, but not necessarily creative ones. Therefore, it is not surprising that many creative people dislike school.

In a narrow-minded, unimaginative environment, being creative can be a disadvantage. A question that has intrigued researchers for centuries is, Does being a creative individual and "different" from other people cause emotional problems or do the emotional problems fuel creativity?

Neuroscientists as well as psychotherapists are spending a lot of time trying to find the answer. Recent discoveries have shown a similarity between certain brain chemicals in schizophrenics and those in artists and other creative individuals.

Thorton Sargent, a biophysicist at Lawrence Berkeley Laboratory of the University of California, for instance, is tracing the disposition of an amphetaminelike molecule closely related to dopamine in the brain. "The thing that is really intriguing is that there is evidence of hallucinatory activity caused by some of the molecules similar to that experienced by schizophrenics," Sargent says. "We have found that some of these molecules actually concentrate in the retina. This high concentration of trace material found in the retina (image-receiving cells at the back of the eye) suggest that visual hallucination may actually originate in the retina. . . .

"The risk of mental illness in every area of creativity is very high whether it be art, music, literature or whatever. The risk of psychosis is very high in the artist. Probably as high as 30 percent."[1]

Dr. Jon Karlsson, an eminent psychiatrist at Napa State Hospital in California, also is investigating whether the same process that produces the creative "high" in an artist can also produce the disrupted perceptions and behavior experienced by the schizophrenic.[2] He points out that a number of highly creative scientists exhibited schizophrenic tendencies. Gregor Mendel, the father of genetics, for example, joined a monastery because he had a nervous breakdown and wanted to get away from the "rigors of having to make a living," as he put it.

Sir Isaac Newton, according to Dr. Karlsson, wrote delusional letters that were classic examples of paranoid schizophrenia. And yet Newton was able to put two observations together in a new way. Dr. Karlsson points out that accumulation of data is not creativity. The creative leap occurs when observed facts are correlated in a new order; and Newton did just that when he observed an apple falling from a tree and saw a common quality in the apple attracted by the earth and the motions of the heavenly bodies.

We'll never know for sure whether Newton really suffered from schizophrenia, but we do have the benefit of his creative genius, the basic laws of gravity. Current research, however, does show an intriguing link between schizophrenia and creativity. When researchers at the University of California gave tests to creative subjects and to schizophrenics, the investigators found that the answers of the two groups were almost identical.

Chances are scientists will ultimately discover that the difference between schizophrenia and creativity may lie merely in the levels of the same neurotransmitters in their brains.

Neurotransmitters are known to be a major factor in another mental illness also associated with creativity— depression. Dr. Karlsson and many other researchers have pointed out that some of the world's great modern poets, writers, and artists have taken their own lives in fits of dejection. Charles Darwin, according to the California research, had classic symptoms of manic-depression, in which there are periodic mood swings from hyperactivity to the depths of despair.

Schizophrenia and depression, of course, have to do with how an individual perceives the world. In the former, the incoming stimuli may be too strong and/or disorganized. In the latter, the input is too weak. In the former, the neurotransmitter dopamine is believed to be involved, and in the latter, the neurotransmitter epinephrine.

Many neuroscientists, particularly neuropsychiatrists, maintain that the famous writers and artists who were mentally ill created despite their abnormal brain chemistry, not because of it. Frederic F. Flach, M.D., a New York psychiatrist, is one who has made a specialty of studying the creative process.[3-4] He maintains: "You do have to be free enough of the norms to see something in a fresh way, and you have to be able to ignore the criticism of the establishment, but usually neuroses and psychoses impede rather than help creativity." He adds that creativity does often follow a period of depression. By its very nature, depression is associated with endings, and because each ending involves starting over, depression can lead to a new beginning.

While there is much yet to be learned about the fascinating correlation between the neurochemistry of mental illness and creativity, what we are concerned with in this book is increasing the potential of the "normal" brain. Creativity is one of the most marvelous products of the "fit brain."

How can you increase your creativity?

There are two major concepts about creativity among neuroscientists. Some believe that almost everyone is capable of great creative achievement, but the potential is used by only a few geniuses among us. Others believe that creativity is something with which you are born and that it cannot be taught or instilled by training any more than left-handedness, perfect pitch, or 20/20 vision can. But while the neurochemical and psychological processes of creativity may be debated, there is no doubt that there are techniques you can master to develop your own novel ways of using your brain, no matter what your age.[5]

First of all, let's consider the current theories about the anatomy of creativity. In the 19th century, researchers concluded that there is a difference in the specialization of the two halves of our brains. The left side is concerned with the spoken language, right-side body control, number skills, written language, reading and reasoning, and our sense of who we are. The right side is involved in left-side body control, music awareness, three-dimensional forms, art awareness, imagination, and intuition. The two sides communicate via a complex switchboard between them—the corpus callosum.

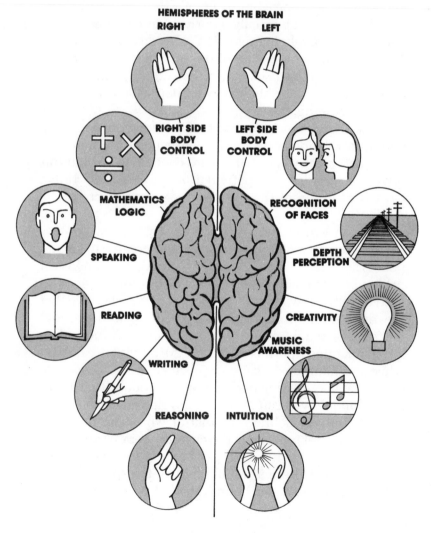

HEMISPHERES OF THE BRAIN

RIGHT   LEFT

RIGHT SIDE BODY CONTROL   LEFT SIDE BODY CONTROL

MATHEMATICS LOGIC   RECOGNITION OF FACES

SPEAKING   DEPTH PERCEPTION

READING   CREATIVITY

WRITING   MUSIC AWARENESS

REASONING   INTUITION

There are neuroscientists who believe that in Western society we emphasize the left side of the brain, thus favoring our scientists and engineers. In fact, there are now courses to teach engineers to make greater use of the right side of their brains so that they can have more fun and intuition and see "global pictures" instead of just parts.[6]

Left and Right Brain
Ask someone a question and observe whether he or she looks to the right or left when answering. If the person looks to the left, he or she is giving you an intuitive or creative answer. If the glance is to the right, that person is giving you a logical or thought-out response.

There are brain researchers who maintain that geniuses in our society subordinate the normally dominant left hemisphere, the seat of logic and linear thinking, to the right hemisphere, the site of intuition and dreaming. Great art, it is now conjectured, may be the product of the artist's right brain–left brain interplay.

Throughout art history, the most important element is usually located in the right half of the picture. Neuroscientists, explaining what the artists have instinctively known, say that when you view a painting, the right hemisphere of your brain is selectively activated and entices your attention toward the left part of the picture. Pictures that correct for this imbalance by having the more important content on the right side are considered the more aesthetically pleasing.[6]

Whether the right or left hemisphere is involved in a particular task seems to be also determined by your previous experience. Musically inexperienced listeners, for instance, recognize melodies better with their left ear (right hemisphere) than with their right, while most concert-level musicians demonstrate a distinct right ear (left hemisphere) advantage. Such findings are leading neuropsychologists to speculate that the right hemisphere processes relatively unfamiliar material, and that as the material becomes more familiar it is taken over by the left hemisphere.

Close to 60 percent of the left-handed people use their cerebral hemispheres the same way that right-handers do, while 40 percent of the lefties reverse the specialization of their brain halves and use their left hemisphere for spatial tasks and their right for language.

Which hemisphere is your dominant one? Write the following paragraph:

> I am looking at my hand as it is writing. Am I left-handed or right-handed? If I am right-handed, is my wrist straight as I am writing? If I am left-handed, is my wrist curled or straight as I am writing?

Dr. Jerre Levy of the Department of Psychology at the University of Chicago found that almost all right-handers keep their wrists straight because their language processing emanates from the opposite (left) side of their brains.[7] When a leftie curls his wrist to write in almost an upside-down hand position, it indicates that he is using the left side of his brain for language processing, just as the straight-wristed right-hander is doing. However, the leftie who keeps his wrist straight while writing is using the opposite side of his brain, the right, for language processing. The curled-wrist position, therefore, is a biological marker indicating that the side of the brain being used for language processing is on the *same side* as the writing hand.

Dr. Levy and her colleagues have reported that those who use the same side of their brain to write and to process language have a slower reaction time when tested, although there has been some controversy about this observation.

Current theory is, nevertheless, that in most people the right side of the brain is the reservoir of creativity. (Exercises to stimulate the right side of the brain are given later in the chapter.)

Since, as we mentioned at the beginning of this chapter, our society in general and our schools in particular subvert creativity, how can we release our natural ability to innovate?

Mining our own preconscious may be one answer.

Dr. Flach points out that psychotherapy can be a creative act because it uncovers new relationships among new and old data in an individual: "The person who is creative has the ability to envision things in different ways to have a fresh outlook. But the source of a creative idea is not the conscious or the subconscious but the preconscious."[8]

According to Dr. Flach and other psychoanalysts:

To be conscious means to be aware and to have a perception of oneself, one's acts, and one's surroundings.
The preconscious includes all ideas, thoughts, past experiences, and other memory impressions that with effort can be consciously recalled.
The subconscious is a state in which mental processes take place without conscious perception.

Dr. Flach explains that when we are *conscious,* we are aware of our surroundings, but we are limited by the pedestrian, literal restrictions of conscious language. In our *subconscious,* our feelings are so buried they are inaccessible. Our painful past experiences and emotions are locked up. In our *preconscious,* however, things are close to the surface. It's our computer data center where we put things together—memories, fantasies, and the vibrations we pick up from other people; we are in touch with ourselves.

The preconscious has been demonstrated under hypnosis. Individuals were asked to observe various objects in a room and then recall them. When they were put under hypnosis, which taps the preconscious, they were able to recall nearly ten times the number of details than at the conscious level.

The creative process itself is said to be a way for the artist to master internal conflicts—disturbing images that are in the subconscious and preconscious as well as the conscious. Dr. Flach maintains that the major need to create, however, is the drive toward finding oneself: "Creativity is not just a product or an act, but a way of viewing and reacting in new and constructive ways. You have to adapt and readapt to your environment at home, at work, and in your relationships. You also have to trust your intuition. Intuition is quite different from impulsiveness. It involves perceiving something along preconscious routes frequently by passing ordinary logic. It is often an artist's or writer's intuition that make masterpieces."

While the psychotherapists, neuroanatomists, and neurochemists are trying to understand the physiologic factors underlying the cognition that produces creativity, they agree that there is little doubt that most of us have a potential for creativity we do not fully develop.

How You Can Increase Your Creativity
The following are basic exercises that have been shown to stimulate areas of your brain that are known to be involved in creativity.
- Name all the kinds of dogs you can.
- Fill in: Her eyes were are green as_____
- Make as many different things out of the circles and squares on the following page as possible.
- Write within three minutes every word you can think of that begins with Y. If you can compete against someone, so much the better. Thinking while competing is a good exercise for the real world.

Uncover and Rid Yourself of Creativity Inhibitors
The process whereby you talk about yourself and delve back into your experiences with a friend or a therapist may unleash your creativity. Psychotherapy can uncover new facts or new relationships among new and old data

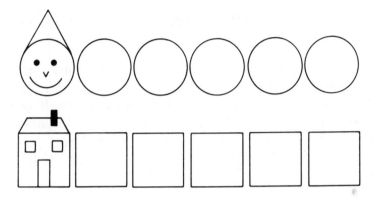

and rid you of inhibitions caused by people and circumstances you faced in the past—that teacher who told you you were inadequate or the need to earn money for necessities are examples. Even simply reminiscing can give you a "fresh outlook."

The following are techniques developed by Dr. Flach, Dr. Morris Stein,[9] and many other psychologists and psychiatrists to help people free themselves from the restrictions of routine and to use their innate creativity to develop new projects, find solutions to problems, and adapt to change. You can use these steps in your own life for whatever it is you wish to create.

① *Prepare yourself.* Do as much reading and talking as you can about what you want to create—a solution, a picture, a new approach to a business. Do your homework.

② *Incubate.* We all want quick solutions, but when the answers don't come right away, put the thought aside. Let it simmer in your subconscious. At a later point, perhaps a week or month later, there will be a breakthrough.

③ *Illuminate.* In cartoons, this is depicted by a light bulb over the head. It is the point when the breakthrough occurs. You let it happen. Something pops into your head and you say, "Ah, that's a good idea."

④ *Test.* Now that you've come up with the creative solution, you have to apply it. If there is a new way to handle your marriage, for example, put it into practice. If you have a new way of creating a sculpture, do it. Dr. Flach says that nobody gets the Nobel Prize for a new idea. One gets it for testing the idea and showing that it works.

⑤ *Distance yourself.* You can do this merely by changing the room in which you are working or your clothes. You can take a "mental excursion" by thinking about a pleasant trip you took or a place you'd like to go. Look at pictures far removed from your ordinary interests or work.

⑥ *Have a variety of leisure pursuits.* Don't spend your leisure time at one avocation, such as tennis or watching TV. Get a variety of experiences. Meet new people. Read new books. First of all, leisure should relax you. It is hard to be creative when you are tense. And by avoiding routine—tennis only or TV only—you gain the stimuli of various people and environments and you use a variety of your muscles and talents. Variety is fertilizer for creativity.

⑦ *Find security.* It is very difficult to be creative if you are worried about survival. You need to find someone on whom you can depend. Anxiety blocks the free flow of creativity.

⑧ *Don't play a role.* If you select a role such as the man-in-the-gray-flannel-suit or the superwoman, you get locked in and can't do things another way.

⑨ *Choose your associates carefully.* If you associate with people who are constantly tearing you down, criticizing you, you won't be able to create.

⑩ *Don't be afraid to be alone.* If you are to be creative, you need time to listen to your inner self instead of someone or something else.

⑪ *Try to turn down your motor.* You need some inactive and quiet time to let your thought processes work. That means daydreaming, a form of mental activity frowned upon by parents and teachers—yet it is useful and may open up new channels. You can also reminisce and allow past successes and failures to flow through your mind for reevaluation.

⑫ *Be disciplined.* It may seem paradoxical, but unstructured environments are not conducive to creativity. You have to have a certain degree of structure in order to be able to create.

⑬ *Keep a pencil and notebook handy.* You can capture fleeting ideas that may later prove to be valuable. You never know what connections may be made between what is novel to you and what you ordinarily have to do.

⑭ *Find your best time.* You are influenced by your biological rhythm. There is a time of day or night when you are at your best. You probably know it, but if you want to make sure, it is probably the time when your body temperature is highest.

⑮ *Find your best place.* Try to remember where you got your best ideas. Some people like to think in a warm bathtub and others while walking or while working with their hands.

16 *Write or tape your frustrations.* When you are feeling frustrated or tied up in knots and the ideas won't come, write or record what is bothering you. It will help "clear the decks" for action.

17 *Farm your brain.* Verbalize or write down as many ideas as you can dig out of your brain. Let your mind wander and consider all sorts of solutions. You can help yourself till the fertile soil by making analogies. For example, "I want to paint a better picture, but it is like squeezing the last bit of toothpaste from the tube."

18 *"Creative dawning."* In this technique (which has been called other names) you put your goal in the center or "sun" (see opposite page) and then try to think of as many ideas as you can—no matter how crazy—that could help you achieve your goal. Put those ideas in the rays around your dawning sun.

19 *Defer judgment.* Really listen to your own thoughts, but don't judge your ideas right away. Don't say, 'That's foolish" or "That won't work." By offering negative adjectives, you block the flow of ideas. Keep coming up with solutions no matter how crazy they may sound. Quantity will eventually produce quality.

20 *Don't be afraid to make mistakes.* If you fail, learn what doesn't work. Try a new approach. If you are not failing, you are not being very creative, because new trails are unmarked and full of pitfalls.

21 *Don't make excuses.* Age, infirmity, and lack of time are frequent reasons given for not being able to create. They are rarely valid. Picasso, at 91, kept art supplies by his bed in case he awoke during the night and had a good idea. He could then capture it on paper. George Bernard Shaw

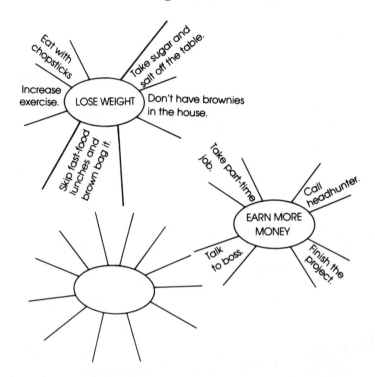

wrote *The Millionairess* in his eighties. The output of composer Gabriel Faure (1845–1924) increased in quantity and quality during his eighth decade of life even in the face of severe sensory impairment.

Bernice Neugarten, Ph.D., one of the first social scientists to devote her career to the study of aging, observed before a congressional hearing in the late 1970s: "People 50 or 60 or 70 are doing things today which they would not and could not have done fifty years ago with social or family approval. Today, persons of these ages return to school for additional education, begin new careers, marry or remarry, reenter the labor market, retire and travel widely or devote themselves entirely to leisure pursuit."[10]

9

Food for Thought

Food fuels your brain and powers its control over your body. Neurotransmitters—those electrochemical messengers sent between nerve cells—are made directly and indirectly from the nutrients you ingest.

What you eat influences the production of the hormones needed by your brain to oversee your body functions, and food provides the vitamins vital to its vitality. Your meals provide substances that your brain requires but cannot make, such as choline and glucose.

Your brain's major fuel is glucose—blood sugar—which is derived from foods, primarily starches and simple sugars. It is present at all times in the blood, usually in an amount maintained within quite a narrow range. Recent studies using the PET Scanner (Positron-Emission Tomography, which traces the mind's workings through chemical "footprints") have shown that the brain's capacity to use glucose also remains pretty stable well into old age if we remain healthy.[1] In contrast, those with Alzheimer's disease, which causes deterioration of the brain and severe memory deficits, show significant impairment in the use of glucose, particularly in the inner areas of their brains.

Although there is a great deal of controversy among scientists about the effects of ingested foods on the brain,

130 .

no one denies that you can change your cognition and mood by what you eat.

SUGAR'S EFFECT ON THE BRAIN

Let's consider sugar first, since it is the major fuel. Directly after you eat a meal, your glucose level rises. Then your pancreas secretes insulin to help move sugar into the cells, and your glucose level drops. If you have hypoglycemia, however, your blood sugar falls to lower than normal levels following a meal, and for reasons that are not always understood, your brain doesn't get enough blood sugar and sends out distress signals.

There are two basic types of hypoglycemia:

(1) *Reactive hypoglycemia,* which occurs about two to four hours after eating, especially if the meal was high in carbohydrates. As the blood sugar drops, the person suddenly experiences dizziness, fatigue, weakness, nervousness, and heart palpitations. These symptoms are not unlike those of an acute anxiety attack. They are the result not of the low blood sugar, however, but of too much of the hormone epinephrine (adrenaline), which is sent to signal the liver to make more glucose.

(2) *Fasting hypoglycemia,* which occurs more slowly and is more rare and serious. It occurs during the night or before breakfast and can be associated with conditions such as alcoholic intake with food; misuse of diabetic drugs; and a serious underlying disorder, such as an insulin-secreting tumor or liver disease.

We all can suffer from hypoglycemia if we suddenly binge on high-calorie carbohydrate meals after eating little throughout the day.

If you do not have a medical condition that causes hypoglycemia but you do have minor problems with maintaining your blood sugar levels and wish to avoid distressing your brain with too little fuel, try the following sensible eating pattern: Avoid sweets, pastries, and sugar-containing drinks such as colas, cocoa, and alcoholic beverages—all of which can cause the blood sugar to drop. Instead of two or three meals a day, eat six small high-protein meals. With more frequent meals, you eat less each time so that rather than having three wide swings upward and downward in your blood sugar, you can maintain it on a more even keel.

Another problem due to sugar is *diabetes*—a condition in which blood sugar levels are too high. It can be treated and damage to the brain and body prevented or greatly reduced. Type II diabetes, which occurs in adulthood, can often be prevented and/or treated merely by dietary control, weight loss, and exercise. Type I diabetes, which is more serious, requires medication to control blood sugar.

Researchers have found that when there are high levels of sugar in the blood—whether or not the patient suffers from diabetes—the severity of brain damage is increased when the supply of blood to the brain is insufficient. In studies of stroke patients, it was found that those with higher blood glucose levels had more permanent nerve and brain damage than those with lower levels; only 43 percent of those with higher levels of blood glucose as compared with 76 percent of those with lower levels were able to return to work.[2]

Blood sugar levels can be better controlled with medications today than ever before. Therefore, to protect your brain against the damage from high blood sugar, have yourself tested for it by your physician periodically, and if it is high, follow your doctor's advice meticulously.

DOES SUGAR MAKE YOU BAD?

Sugar levels in the blood not only affect your brain cells and blood vessels but your behavior. There are a number of studies, some of them quite controversial, that conclude that a sugary, refined-food diet can cause aggression.

Barbara Reed, an Ohio probation officer, advocated in 1971 dietary reform for all her probationers. She had found that when she herself eliminated sugary junk foods, white flour, and canned foods from her meals, she felt much better. She reported that clients who followed her instructions reported feeling better, more energetic, and more emotionally stable. But what really intrigued other law-enforcement agencies was that the rate of recidivism among her charges plunged.

Stephen Schoenthaler, director of the social justice program at California State College at Stanislaus, began a study of juveniles at Virginia's Tidewater Detention Center in Chesapeake during 1980 to see if there was a correlation between sugar and antisocial behavior. Restricting white sugar and substituting fruit juice for colas and honey for table sugar resulted in a 45 percent drop in antisocial behavior among the inmates.

Diana Fishbein, a University of Baltimore criminologist, also explored diet and violence and explained why the results may be so spectacular. She pointed out that the brain uses 50 percent of all the glucose in the blood. Therefore, when blood sugar levels are too low, the brain cannot function well and, consequently, behavior is affected. She said that research suggests that low blood sugar may contribute to irritability, headaches, agitation, frustration, and explosive behavior. It is ironic, she added, that the more sugar one consumes, the lower one's blood sugar tends to be.

Schoenthaler reasons that chronic deficiencies in elements essential to glucose metabolism, such as zinc, iron, phosphorous, and magnesium, may contribute to deprivation of chemical energy needed by the brain for intellectual functioning. He points out that if there is an energy shortage, the limbic system, the most primitive part of the brain, gets priority since it controls involuntary muscle responses, such as those for breathing and pumping blood. The region also seems to control emotions. Therefore, he speculates, if the brain is denied sufficient energy, the region sacrificed might be that which contributes to reasoning.[3]

Studies done with adults show that meals with high sugar levels not only make them sluggish but interfere with their concentration. Dr. Bonnie Spring of Harvard University found that adults had difficulty performing a simple speech test after eating a sherbetlike high-carbohydrate snack. The decline was especially marked for those over 40. Her tests also showed differences in the way men and women felt after eating the "sherbet": Women had a more pronounced reaction and reported feeling lethargic and sleepy, while men simply reported feeling calmer.[4]

So, overloading the blood with sugar can cause a paradoxical drop in blood sugar levels. Skipping meals can also cause blood sugar levels to be too low for the brain. Dr. Ernesto Pollitt of the University of Texas worked with a group of children and had half of them skip breakfast while the other half ate a meal of waffles and syrup, milk, and orange juice. By late morning, those who had eaten breakfast made fewer errors solving problems than the children who skipped breakfast.[5]

HOW BAD DOES IT HURT?

Diet may not only affect how we think and behave but how we feel pain. Pain is basically a protective mechanism. The brain senses pain signals designed to make us aware that something is wrong in some area of our bodies and that action must be taken to correct it. Unfortunately, even after we are informed by our pain that something is amiss, those uncomfortable pain signals may continue to be received by our brains. Pain signals may be dampened by controlling our intake of sugar and salt.

G. Frank Lawlis, Ph.D., and his colleagues at North Texas State University's Clinical Ecology and Chronic Pain Patient Clinic, reported at the 1984 American Psychological Association meeting the results of studies involving sugar and salt. Dr. Lawlis said that when sugar enters the bloodstream at a very high rate, the pancreas produces a rush of insulin to stabilize the levels in the bloodstream and, as a result of the overproduction, the blood glucose is washed out and drops lower than before the sugar was ingested. The temporary high blood sugar and insulin level, however, may produce a feeling of relief. Some patients perceive this stage as feeling high and happier, while others relate it to a state of increased relaxation. It does not last very long. Since the brain uses glucose in the production of its own self-made pain-killers and pleasure producers, the endorphins, pain symptoms and a depressed mood may appear or worsen when blood sugar levels become unbalanced.[6]

The second food substance that may greatly affect the brain's perception of pain, the Texas researchers maintain, is sodium in the form of salt. Physiologically, sodium makes the interior of the blood vessels soggy, producing higher blood pressure. If you have an inflammation anywhere in your body or swelling, increased pressure will cause the pain to get worse. Scar tissue would also be affected by the same mechanism.

Some foods, the Texans maintain, can help decrease pain. Tryptophan, an amino acid that we discuss in more detail later in this chapter, is a stimulant of the brain's natural pain-killing and pleasure-producing chemicals, the endorphins. Bananas, for example, have high levels of tryptophan as well as high levels of potassium, an element that when depleted causes muscle spasms. Muscle spasms, of course, can cause pain. Other foods that produce good results are almonds, melons, and grapes. The pain researchers also recommend potatoes and pastas as foods that help balance blood sugar. They appear to break down into blood sugar very slowly over the course of a day, thus helping to keep blood sugar levels in balance. Rice cakes, popcorn, and water help a patient to feel full. Water in copious amounts is recommended because as muscles exercise, they give off lactic acid, which causes soreness. Water can help get rid of the lactic acid.

A small amount of white wine may be beneficial for pain and stress. Beer, however, can be a problem because of its high sodium levels. Highly distilled liquors, such as gin, vodka, and whiskey, have a disastrous effect, the Texans have found. They speculate that it is because alcohol disintegrates the brain's pain-killing system, the endorphins.

ALCOHOL AND THE BRAIN

It has been known for a long time that alcohol destroys brain cells. In fact, the brains of chronic alcoholics are softer than normal. It has been shown in animals that an alcohol diet for five months produces pathological changes in both the organization and the activity of nerve cells, in particular the brain structure called the hippocampus, which is believed to participate in the processing of information for storage into memory. Although alcohol probably exerts widespread effects on the nervous system, the fact that alcoholics often show severe memory disorders provides a clue that alcohol may exert its primary toxic effects on the hippocampus.[7] Current research on alcohol and the brain suggests that the symptoms alcoholics suffer are not similar to those experienced by normal people as they age but to those suffered by persons who have brain damage.[8]

Most people experience alcoholic intoxication sometime in their lives. New research is explaining intoxication, tolerance, and withdrawal.

Our brains have been found to have receptors for their own self-produced opiates, the endorphins. The endorphins fit into these receptors like pegs into pegboards. These same receptors also act as depots for other opiates or psychoactive drugs we ingest. After long-term exposure to alcohol, the number of opiate receptors in the brain apparently increases.

Michael Charness, M.D., assistant professor of neurology at the University of California at San Francisco, and his colleagues examined the ability of the receptor for one of the endorphins, methionine enkephalin, to receive it. Methionine enkephalin has a soothing message and if it cannot bind to the appropriate receptor, it cannot deliver it. Although alcohol initially inhibited the endorphin's binding, the researchers found that nerve cells adapted to this inhibition by increasing the number of methionine enkephalin–binding sites. This fits in with the common observation that chronic alcoholics and drug abusers have to keep increasing their intake of psychoactive substances in order to get an effect. The additional receptors were first detected after 18 hours of exposure to alcohol; and after four days, the number of opiate receptors was 85 percent higher. When alcohol was withdrawn, the number of receptors remained elevated for one to two days before returning to normal levels.

When alcohol is abruptly taken away, therefore, it leaves a lot of extra receptors that it no longer inhibits, and the result is believed to account for such symptoms as alcohol withdrawal seizures.

THE CAFFEINE CHARGE

Caffeine, even more than alcohol, is a substance widely consumed for its behavioral effects—stimulation and abatement of drowsiness and fatigue. It quickly makes its presence felt in the brain and other organs in the body. Caffeine occurs naturally in several plant components, including the coffee bean, tea leaf, kola nut, cacao seed, and ilex leaf. The average American consumes 2 to 3 milligrams per 35⅕ ounces of his or her body weight per day; many consume more than 10 mg. About 75 percent of the caffeine ingested is in coffee. One cup of coffee contains between 50 and 150 mg. Caffeine is also present in soft drinks and in several over-the-counter medications, including analgesics, appetite suppressants, and stimulants.

Readings on the electroencephalogram after caffeine is administered are similar to those seen during normal physiological arousal and to those produced by direct stimulation of areas in the brain stem believed to play a major role in wakefulness.[9] The alertness-enhancing effects of caffeine are apparent at low doses that have few other discernible effects on body organs. In higher doses, say, 10 to 15 mg., caffeine can produce nervousness and insomnia; very much higher doses, say, 200 mg., can produce seizures and death.

Caffeine, which is readily absorbed, affects the central nervous system, respiratory and cardiovascular systems, smooth and skeletal muscles, gastrointestinal secretion, the rate of urine formation, and the basal metabolic rate. The brain, however, seems to be the most sensitive to caffeine. The time it takes to fall asleep is doubled in some people by a single serving of 1 to 2 mg. of caffeine. One can see the alertness effect of caffeine in those who regularly consume it. In those who are not normally coffee drinkers, however, the same dose can cause irritability and nervousness. Caffeine deprivation can cause the same symptoms in regular users.

Caffeine's half-life—the time it is active—in smokers is three to four hours instead of five to six hours. The known association between increased caffeine consumption and cigarette smoking could depend, in part, on the fact that more caffeine is needed to obtain an effect on a smoker's mood.

Since caffeine produces arousal, you would expect that it increases blood flow, but a cup or two of coffee actually decreases blood flow to the brain significantly. In fact, it has been used for that purpose in treating migraines, in which the blood vessels of the brain are distended.

Another paradoxical effect of coffee is that it is sometimes used to test children for hyperactivity. For many who are truly hyperactive, coffee acts to calm them down instead of stimulate them. The reasons are not clear, but similar results have been observed with pharmaceutical stimulants.

Caffeine is believed to affect the brain receptors for adenosine, a chemical secreted by the liver. Adenosine administration to animals can produce sedation, irregular heartbeat, low blood pressure, low temperature, and other heart and vascular actions. These are generally just the opposite effects produced by one or two cups of coffee.

THE MEANING OF AMINOS

Amino acids derived from the protein we eat are the starting materials for our brain's chemical messengers, the neurotransmitters. Diets deficient in protein have been reported to cause permanent damage to the intelligence of the young and to affect the memory and cognition of the elderly.[10]

There are three amino acids that are being intensively |

studied for their effects on the brain: tyrosine, tryptophan, and acetylcholine.

Tyrosine is not considered an *essential* amino acid because it can be manufactured by the body from another amino acid, phenylalanine. When the enzyme that transforms phenylalanine to tyrosine is not active because of a hereditary defect, the serious disease known as phenylketonuria (PKU) occurs. PKU causes mental retardation.

Tyrosine is a building block for the nerve messengers epinephrine and norepinephrine, as well as for the thyroid hormones and melanin, the skin and hair pigment. Norepinephrine and epinephrine are neurotransmitters involved in strong emotions and alertness. Thyroid hormones are necessary for normal metabolism of food and also strongly influence the brain and behavior.

Dr. Alan J. Gelenberg, a psychiatrist at Harvard Medical School, reported that some depressed patients who took tablets of tyrosine, in addition to their regular diet, improved. However, the tyrosine provided solely by a high-protein diet did not have the same benefit.[11]

When tryptophan, another amino acid, is not available to the body at sufficient levels, it enhances the progress of the B vitamin–deficiency disease pellagra. The condition, which is manifested by mental and nerve disorders, is treated by restoring nicotinic acid, a B vitamin, in the diet. Nicotinic acid can be made from tryptophan.

Tryptophan was first isolated from milk in 1901. It is believed to work in partnership with tyrosine to produce the brain chemicals serotonin, dopamine, and norepinephrine. The theory is that nerve cell communication by these powerful brain chemicals can be affected by the availability of their building blocks, tryptophan and tyrosine. Since these two amino acids are supplied by the diet, the possibility is also considered that diet-induced alterations in blood levels of tryptophan and tyrosine can affect serotonin, dopamine, and norepinephrine, and thus the brain and behavior.

Eating carbohydrates raises the level of tryptophan, and this is why a warm glass of milk or sugary, starchy foods may work to make you sleepy. Dr. Ernest Hartmann of Tufts University School of Medicine has studied the effects of extra doses of tryptophan on groups of normal people and mild insomniacs. Those who took tryptophan tablets fell asleep sooner. This suggests that eating carbohydrate-rich foods, which raise tryptophan levels, might offer similar relief for those troubled by insomnia.

Dr. Michael Yogman of Children's Hospital Medical Center in Boston has also shown the sleep-inducing effects of tryptophan. He reported that babies go to sleep faster when a solution of sugar and tryptophan is added to their bottles, but warned against mothers doing their own experimenting with tryptophan.[12]

A high-protein diet that contains a lot of tyrosine and tryptophan has been used to try to increase the level of dopamine and serotonin in patients with neurological and psychiatric disorders thought to involve these brain neurotransmitters. Dopamine is necessary to movement and serotonin is believed to inhibit aggressive behaviors and be involved in the sleep-wake cycle. Doctors who are investigating the amino acids for this purpose say that thus far, it looks promising.[13] On the other hand, protein restriction on alternate feeding days seems to prolong the lives of animals and reportedly retards the loss of their brains' dopamine receptors.

Perhaps the greatest concentration of research concerns choline, a substance that is found either alone or as part of lecithin and the B vitamin complex. It is a precursor or building block of acetylcholine, the neurotransmitter involved in stimulation of the nerves. The nerves that produce acetylcholine are believed to undergo degeneration and to be a cause of the cognitive dysfunction in Alzheimer's. Acetylcholine is also believed to be involved in other memory problems commonly associated with aging.

When mice were fed choline-enriched diets over a period of several months, the type of memory deficits typically seen in old mice did not occur. It appeared that prolonged dietary choline treatment somehow enabled the mice to form new long-term memories more efficiently than old mice not on the diet.[14]

In humans, thus far, a choline-enriched diet—meat, fish, dairy products, and grains—has not seemed to help those suffering from memory problems. But researchers are studying the long-term effects of supplements of choline and lecithin, the building blocks of acetylcholine. A great deal of research is in progress to determine whether drugs can enhance the effect on brain function of choline in the diet.

A deficiency of D-phenylalanine has been linked to the destruction of nerve coverings, which interferes with transmission and produces incoordination and other problems such as those seen in multiple sclerosis. It is also being studied as a contributing factor in some forms of depression.[15]

Obviously, there are a lot of contradictory reports and many unanswered questions about the effects of amino acids on the brain, but it is one of the most exciting and potentially rewarding areas of brain research.

VITAMINS AND BRAIN FUNCTION

Vitamins—which were named for the Latin "vita," meaning life—are vital to the proper functioning of the brain and act as helpers for the neurotransmitters. It is believed by many gerontologists that one of the problems with cognition in the elderly is that they suffer from subclinical malnutrition.

One researcher has dubbed the condition the "tea and white bread syndrome." He explained that because of physical disability or fear of crime, many older people living alone eat only tea and white bread, which keeps a long time. They consequently suffer from malnutrition.[16]

Memory problems may also cause malnutrition and vitamin deficiency because victims may forget to take prescribed vitamins or may prepare meals inadequately. Researcher James S. Goodwin, M.D., and his colleagues at the University of New Mexico School of Medicine, writing in the *Journal of the American Medical Association*, reported a correlation between low blood levels of vitamin C, B12, riboflavin, and folic acid and lower scores on standard tests for memory and nonverbal abstract thinking ability.[17]

Vitamin deficiencies—in particular, deficit of the B vitamins thiamine, niacin, and B12—are relatively common among older people, sometimes due to diet inadequacies and sometimes due to malabsorption. When monkeys were deprived of the B vitamin thiamine, they exhibited a pattern of impairment in learning and in recognition of highly familiar items reminiscent of certain memory deficits shown by patients with brain damage and memory deficits due to alcoholism. Postmortem exams in the B-deficient monkeys showed nerve degeneration in the basal ganglia, the thalamus, the brain stem, and the cerebellum.

The B vitamins are necessary for good nerve function and appetite. But like other vitamins and the amino acids, self-dosing with large amounts is unwise. Cases have been reported of nerve damage due to excessive intake of a B vitamin. A diet sufficient in the B vitamins is certainly recommended. Foods that are high in Vitamin B12 are liver, meat, milk and dairy foods. Foods high in folate, another B vitamin, include liver, lentils, dry beans, asparagus, green leafy vegetables, fish, meats, wheat products, and broccoli.

Deficiencies in iron, zinc, and calcium have also been correlated with problems in cognition.

Iron was found to help the cognitive performance of mildly deficient 3- to 6-year-olds in Cambridge, Massachusetts. After being given iron supplements, the children improved on three discrimination learning tasks. It was shown that bringing their iron levels to normal had a great beneficial effect on their ability to pay attention. Again, iron should not be taken unless a physician has tested you and prescribed it.[18]

Calcium has long been suspected as a cause of changes in the structure and function of nerve cells and in the physiology of learning. One implication is that diets deficient in calcium severely disrupt or handicap learning.[19]

A diet deficient in zinc was found to cause memory and learning impairment in the offspring of laboratory rats fed the diets during pregnancy and suckling periods.[20] A report in the British medical journal *Lancet* also cited zinc as a factor in the onset of genetically based senility. Foods that are high in zinc include meat, oysters, nuts, liver, and wheat germ.

A diet deficient in protein during pregnancy and breast feeding has been correlated with irreparable damage to intelligence in children.[21] Meats, eggs, and legumes are high in protein.

THE FAT CONNECTION

The elevation of "rancid fat" in the blood and tissues of animals has generally been considered one of the factors that speeds the process of aging and increases the prevalence of cerebral and cardiovascular disease. It is also believed that diet and exercise can lower blood fats.

In animal studies, an egg yolk extract containing lecithin and special fats, called *active lipid*, improved mildly impaired memory in alcoholics and eased withdrawal symptoms in drug addicts, according to Dr. David Samuel, head of the Center for Neurosciences and Behavior

Research at the Weitzman Institute of Science, Rehovat, Israel. At this writing, researchers at five United States medical centers were awaiting FDA approval to begin clinical trials with active lipid.

As aging occurs, increasing cholesterol accumulation renders the brain cells less flexible and probably less permeable, altering the activity of neurotransmitters involved in memory. Active lipid, it is suggested, extracts cholesterol from membranes, restoring their fluidity. Biochemical studies of aged, memory-impaired rats injected with it showed increased neurotransmitter capability.

BRAIN POISONS

So far in this chapter, we have described mostly what happens to the brain when there is a deficiency. But another area, and one that is filled with even more controversy, concerns those substances we ingest that irritate or may poison brain cells. Among them are contaminants such as mycotoxins and aflatoxins produced by mold and present in raw agricultural products, such as wheat and peanuts, and shellfish poisons and industrial pollutants.

Chemicals added to our food supply are often not adequately tested for potential neurotoxicity. Among those that do show potential for adversely affecting the nervous system are aspartame, an increasingly popular sweetener; erythrosine, Red Dye No. 3; and a material that migrates into the food from the paper in packaging, polyacrylimide. Polyacrylimide is also used to wash fruit to keep it "fresh" in transit and in the manufacture of sugar. Polyacrylimide has been shown to cause changes not only in the brain but in the kidney, liver, and testes.[22]

Aspartame was determined to be safe for the food supply by the Food and Drug Administration and entered the market in 1981. But it is not safe for those with an intolerance to phenylalanine, one of its components (see page

140). It may also not be safe in combination with glutamate, a food additive used as a flavor enhancer.

It is known that when aspartame is given in certain dosages and routes of administration, it can cause lesioning of the brain in animals. The question remains at what blood level is there a reasonable probability that humans are at risk.

When given together with glutamate, used in the flavor enhancer MSG, aspartame produced lesions in the hypothalamus of newborn animals. (The hypothalamus is the control center for the body's metabolism and hormonal functioning.) Aspartic acid, a constituent in aspartame, and glutamic acid, an ingredient in monosodium glutamate, are capable of inducing lesions in the hypothalamus in animals. They are about equal in potency and the effects have been found to be stronger when they are combined.

THE FEINGOLD CONTROVERSY

In 1975, Dr. Benjamin Feingold, a San Francisco pediatrician, published his thesis on behavioral disorders in children. He claimed dramatic success in alleviating hyperactivity by placing patients on a diet devoid of artificial food, natural salicylates, and color additives.[23] While many parents confirmed the merit of his recommendations, they remained the object of controversy among his peers. The most recent studies do not present final answers. The evidence to date seems to show that there may be a "subpopulation" of children who are sensitive to food colorings and salicylates.

However, six years after Dr. Feingold introduced his theory, it was reported by National Institutes of Health researchers that Red Dye No. 3, erythrosine, may interfere with the neurotransmitters of the brain. There are

81,000 pounds of Red Dye No. 3 consumed a year. It was reported earlier that erythrosine may affect the thyroid. Evidence exists in both animal and human studies that thyroid dysfunction may evoke neurological symptoms, emotional swings, hyperactivity, and irritability.[24]

FOOD ALLERGY AND THE BRAIN

The entire subject of food allergy is a controversial one. There is even a debate over how to test for it. The effect of a food allergy on the brain is difficult to determine. There is no doubt that if you are allergic to corn, wheat, eggs, or milk, and you ingest one of your allergens, you will not feel well and may be irritable or foggy. Allergists report that often when the offending foods are removed, the vertigo, nausea, eye problems, and hearing loss suffered by a number of allergic patients are also removed.[25]

John W. Crayton, M.D., associate professor of psychiatry at the University of Chicago, reported in 1985, after studying foods and cognitive behavior for more than two years, that a sizable literature suggests that adverse reactions to foods can contribute to behavior dysfunction but that clear demonstrations of adverse behavioral reactions to foods are not yet available.[26]

Dr. Crayton noted that there have been a number of studies, for instance, linking wheat ingestion in genetically predisposed individuals to schizophrenia. He pointed out that epidemiological studies suggest that schizophrenia is seldom seen in cultures in which wheat consumption is low, but the incidence rises when wheat is introduced into the culture: "Support for the wheat-schizophrenia connection comes from studies' suggestion that the incidence of antibodies to components of wheat in schizophrenics is higher than in non-schizophrenics and that fragments of wheat gluten have been shown to enter the brains of experimental animals." However, studies in which schizophrenics have been put on wheat-free diets showed no effect—perhaps, Dr. Crayton muses, because once the damage is done by the wheat-schizophrenia connection, it is irreversible, or perhaps because the connection is not valid.

Dr. Crayton also pointed out in his report that many studies have linked depression to allergy. He notes that increasing the amount of carbohydrates in the diet indirectly increases the amount of serotonin, which is in low supply in depressed people. This may explain why certain depressed patients have a craving for carbohydrates. They may, instinctively, be trying to raise the level of serotonin in their brains.

Just how certain foods may adversely affect the transmission of nerve chemicals or affect the brain cells themselves is a fertile field for research. In the meantime, if you believe you are suffering from a behavior dysfunction related to food intolerance and you have other symptoms of allergy, it would be prudent to have a medical evaluation and treatment of the allergy.

If you have food complaints and no other diagnosed medical condition, then keep a food diary. By using a simple elimination diet, you may be able to pinpoint your offending foods.[27]

MEDICATIONS AND THE MIND

The subject of drugs and the brain could fill several books, but we must mention certain drugs in common use that cause problems in cognition. Among those well known to sometimes fog the mind are psychoactives, including sedatives, hypnotics, tranquilizers, marijuana, cocaine, and lithium; medications for high blood pressure; anticonvulsants, barbiturates, and drugs that affect the neuro-

transmitter acetylcholine, such as atropine; and antispas-
modics and the newer ulcer drugs. Among others that are
known to have marked affects on the ability to think
clearly are narcotics, steroids, digitalis, diuretics, anti-
inflammatories, and disulfiram, the drug taken to make
alcoholics sick when they drink liquor.

So, in order to nourish and protect your brain, eat a
well-balanced diet. You could take one multivitamin pill
per day to ensure that you are getting all the vitamins you
need. The fewer man-made chemicals you ingest as food
additives, liquor, and drugs, the less your chance of caus-
ing your brain problems. Do you really need that "flavor
enhancer" or diet soda? Or that ulcer pill?

THE BRAIN'S APPETITE CENTER

If you have a stubborn problem with your weight, brain
researchers are working on that, too. Investigators at
Tufts and Temple universities and the National Institute
of Mental Health have discovered that by giving genetically obese mice and rats nalaxone, a drug that counteracts endorphins, the mice stopped overeating. The researchers conclude that their data suggests that beta
endorphin in the master gland, the pituitary, may play a
role in the development of the overeating and obesity
syndrome.[28]

There are other researchers working on identifying the
chemicals that turn on and off the "appetite-regulating
center in the hypothalamus." Many self-made substances
have been considered, among them, the neurotransmitter dopamine, the endorphins, and the fatty acids. The
suspects for stimulating appetite include the neurotransmitters norepinephrine and adenosine; the hormones insulin and thyrotrophin releasing factor, as well as an
amino acid active in the brain, GABA (Gamma amino
butyric acid).

As the mysteries of the brain and its appetite center unravel, there may prove to be easier means of controlling your appetite. In the meantime, you'll just have to use your brain to regulate what you feed it.

10

Protecting Your Brain
From Stress

Your brain and your body converse with electrochemical signals. There is a sensitive *biofeedback* between them. Your brain says one thing and your body responds. Your body makes a suggestion and your brain answers.

Neuroscientists are rapidly becoming able to decode these conversations. They already know a great deal about how illness, injury, inactivity, and emotional upsets may garble the messages. They are confirming what witch doctors have known all along—thoughts emanating from your brain can cure or kill your body.

Your brain has a built-in chemical alarm system so that when it perceives danger in the environment, it can send signals to ready your body to fight or flee. The key word is *perceives* because something may be stressful to you that may not bother someone else and vice versa.

Stress, which can be either threatening or pleasurable, causes a reported one thousand chemical and physical changes in your brain and body.[1] For example, stress stimulates the production of hormones, those powerful substances manufactured by endocrine glands to orchestrate body functions. Blood levels of the hormones epinephrine (adrenaline), norepinephrine, cortisol, growth hormone, and glucagon, for example, rise under stress. These endocrine products speed metabolism. Other hormones that increase under stress include ADH (antidiuretic hormone), which enhances water reabsorption into the bloodstream; aldosterone, which increases salt retention by the body, and thus water retention; oxytocin, which induces muscle contractions; and renin and angiotensin, which play a role in blood pressure elevation.

On the other hand, certain hormones are suppressed during stress, including insulin, needed to regulate blood sugar; thyroid hormone, which regulates metabolism; and the male sex hormone testosterone. In the female, sex hormones fall out of synchrony under stress and can cause the menstrual cycle to become irregular or absent.

All of the hormones mentioned above normally regulate specific physiological functions that help maintain the body in exquisite balance. When the body is stressed for short periods of time, the effects of stress hormones in a healthy person may be transient. However, when the stress response is prolonged, then the persistent elevation of some hormones and suppression of others can have deleterious effects on the body, including increased blood levels of cholesterol and blood-clotting factors and an increase in blood pressure.

Recent scientific studies have concluded that from 75 to 90 percent of the ills that afflict us are due to stress. For example, young men—aged 28 to 35—working on the man-to-the-moon project at the Kennedy Space Center in the 1960s had a 50 percent higher incidence of cardiovascular disorders and sudden death than did age and sex-matched controls. The frenzied pace, national attention, and manpower cuts produced high stress and frustration levels.

More and more evidence is being gathered to prove that stress depresses the body's defense system. A team at Mt. Sinai Medical Center in New York City, for instance, found that the immune function in husbands of terminally ill breast cancer patients was affected and that susceptibility to disease was at the height three months after the wives died. Most of the widowers' immune systems returned to prebereavement levels within six months.[2]

Stress can even affect the unborn. The hippocampus, a seahorse-shaped area involved in stress responses, has the most binding sites for stress hormones in the brain. Researchers now theorize that when a pregnant woman is exposed to environmental stress, the raised levels of stress hormones in her blood may permanently alter her fetus's hippocampus and thus affect her offspring's response to stress in adulthood. This has been proven to be true in rats whose mothers were stressed during pregnancy.[3]

Stress may prematurely age the adult brain. National Institute on Aging grantee Philip Landfield of the Bowman Gray School of Medicine points out that the brain deterioration seen in older people and that seen in younger people with Cushing's Syndrome, a rapid and premature form of aging associated with high levels of adrenal (stress) hormones, are quite similar. Over the years, Dr. Landfield has found that the blood levels of adrenal hormones in experimental animals correlate significantly with the degree of age-related changes in the brain.[4]

This seems quite logical when you consider that the brain structures that receive and send "emotional" information are called, collectively, the limbic system. One portion about the size of a half dollar, the amygdala, is involved in rage, anger, and fear behaviors. The nearby hippocampus, as noted, is the target area of the adrenal gland's stress hormones, which prepare the body for fight or flight. The continuous bombardment of stress hormones on the brain appears to kill off some of the stress hormone receptors in the hippocampus.[5] As a result, researchers believe, the hippocampus's ability to shut off the system weakens. Thus, through a feedback circuit, the brain's limbic system, the control center of emotions, gradually destroys itself.

While there is yet much to learn about this process, there seems to be little doubt that stress can kill brain cells. One of the most graphic examples of the physical effects of stress on the brain was reported in the November 18, 1982, issue of *The New England Journal of Medicine.* Danish doctors described how they took computerized X-rays (CAT scans) of young men between 24 and 39 years of age who had been victims of political torture. The doctors found that the young men had premature "aging of their brains." All had been healthy and intelligent before being tortured, but their brains were seen on the X-rays to be atrophied. During examinations, the men's ability to concentrate and their memories were found to be impaired. The former prisoners suffered headaches, anxiety, depression, numbness, sleep disturbances, and sexual dysfunction.[6]

The Danish doctors said that the tortured men had symptoms similar to the social and mental complications experienced by victims of concentration camps during World War II. The young men's brains probably had been permanently damaged by stress chemicals secreted when they were tortured.

Torture and experience in concentration camps are extreme forms of stress. But in studies by researchers with the support of the National Institute on Aging, it has been found that if a person does not cope well with everyday stresses, physical problems that shorten life can result.

National Institute on Aging grantee Richard S. Lazarus, working at the University of California at Berkeley, assessed the responses of 100 men and women, 45 to 64 years of age, to daily stresses as well as major life events. Subjects kept a daily log and responded to questionnaires and interviews about sources of stress, from minor annoyances to major problems, and how they felt—happy, guilty, or fearful, for example.[7]

Lazarus found that the frequency of the irritations of everyday life—such as traffic jams or broken appointments or having to rush—as well as the uplifts, were more powerful predictors of psychological and physical health and morale than were major life events.

But, as many others have pointed out, it is not what you meet in daily life so much as how you meet it that really counts. Lazarus found that a subject's view of a problem had an important impact on coping. Participants who felt they could change a situation tended to use problem-solving techniques rather than emotional responses such as seeking sympathy, feeling bad, or blaming themselves. In other words, they used their heads to solve their problems instead of fretting about them.

How you cope, therefore, affects how old your brain is physiologically. Furthermore, there is growing scientific conjecture that brain aging may act as a "pacemaker" for other forms of aging, particularly through the deregulation of hormones that act on the central nervous system.

THE STRESS OF PAIN AND THE BRAIN

Pain is a common and powerful stress, as the victims of torture mentioned above graphically illustrate. Just as fear prepares us to fight or flee, pain signals our brains that something is damaging our bodies. The nerve endings that respond to pain are called nociceptors—from the Greek "noci," meaning noxious. These nociceptors are present in the skin, in sheath tissue surrounding muscles, in internal organs, and in the membranes around the bone and around the cornea of the eye.

There are two levels of response. The first takes place almost as a reflex: You touch your toe to bathwater that is too hot and you withdraw it instantly. Then there are aches and longer-lasting pains. In the first instance, the swift pain message is carried by thin myelinated (coated) fibers. In the second instance, unmyelinated, slow-conducting fibers produce a diffuse, nagging pain.

The fibers of the fast pathway make direct connections with the thalamus, where they are next to the fibers that project to motor and sensory areas of the higher brain, the cortex. This allows you to discriminate exactly where the injury is, how serious the damage, and how long it has been going on.

The fibers of the slow pathway project to many areas of the brain, including the hypothalamus, the thalamus, and the "emotional" areas of the limbic system. It is believed that the fast system gets us out of danger quickly and that the slow system reminds us to take it easy, we have an injury.

There is also a neurotransmitter that is the subject of a great deal of research today, Substance P, a nerve chemical that rapidly builds up after injury. When present in abundance at one segment of the spinal cord, the pain impulses arriving at that segment are enhanced and augmented in their transmission toward the brain. Substance P has also been found in the brain cells, so it probably has functions besides the transmission of pain impulses.

Neuroimmunologist Donald G. Payan, M.D., assistant professor of medicine at the University of California at San Francisco, reported at the 1985 American Association for the Advancement of Science meeting in Los Angeles that he has traced radioactive- and fluorescent-labeled Substance P. He found that it binds most readily with "Helper T Cells," a type of white blood cell that stimulates the body's immune system. He and other researchers believe that Substance P may be involved in autoimmune diseases such as arthritis and allergies where the body's defenses are overactive and injure tissue.[8]

The endorphins, as mentioned many times in this book,

are our own self-produced neurotransmitters that counteract pain and other stress once we have recognized the
danger. If there were no such system, we would be unable
to think to save ourselves or to do something about the
cause of pain. The endorphin-producing brain cells are
logically concentrated in the limbic system, that part of
the brain closely linked with strong emotion. This apparent connection between natural pain-relieving substances and the brain's emotional centers led researchers
to wonder if it could explain the placebo effect. (The term
placebo, from the Latin "I shall please," signifies a medi-
cally inert substance, such as a sugar pill or a saline injection, that is given to patients who think they are receiving
a potent medicine.)

Patients undergoing the extraction of wisdom teeth, a
painful process, volunteered for a test of the placebo
effect. Scientists administered morphine postoperatively
to one group, and injected saline into another group.
They found that 33⅓ percent of those receiving the inert
saline injection had a dramatic reduction in pain. Then
the scientists administered doses of the drug naloxone,
which is known to interfere with the body's production of
endorphins. Those people whose pain had been relieved
by the placebo injection immediately developed shooting
pains. This proved, as far as the researchers were concerned, that those volunteers who were given saline shots
and had relief of pain received the benefit of their own
increased endorphin activity. It also became clear that the
placebo effect, far from being a mind-over-matter mys-
tery, has a definite basis in matter—the chemicals of the
brain.

And, like morphine, the body's own morphinelike
chemicals may cause an addiction. Bessel A. Van der Kilk,
M.D., professor of psychiatry at Harvard Medical School,
and other researchers have shown that prolonged stress,
like the administration of opiates, activates the opiate

receptors in animal brains. When stressed animals received naloxone, which counteracts opiates, or are removed from stress, they develop opiate withdrawal symptoms. This has led to the conclusion that chronically stressed animals may become physically dependent on self-made opiods that are released by the brain to counteract pain and other stresses.[9]

Edgar Wilson, M.D., and Carol Schneider, Ph.D., of the University of Colorado, suggested at the Biofeedback Society of America meeting on April 16, 1985, that one cause of chronic pain may be due to the brain being bombarded by painful sensory inputs from one area of the body over a prolonged period of time. It then tends to become more and more sensitive to those inputs because its self-made opiod supply may become depleted.

Another cause of chronic pain, according to Wilson and Schneider, may be that the cerebellum, which controls movement, develops an irregular movement pattern because the affected muscles are out of synchrony.

They point out that each of us has a holding side of our bodies and a pivot side—usually the dominant side of the brain determines this. If you are right-handed, you are most likely to stand on your right foot when talking and pivot on your left side when you move.[10]

The difference between chronic-pain patients and people who routinely run two or three miles a day, they found, was a marked difference in movement pattern. The pain patients tended to shuffle along, with their shoulders thrust forward, their heads down, their toes turning slightly inward; the general orientation of body movement was from side to side. Runners, instead, had a more vertical orientation of movement. Their shoulders were held back, as well as their heads. The runners, however, leaned into their walks rather than resisting the next step.

The Colorado researchers said that you can prevent

painful "trigger points" in your muscles by working on the symmetry of your movement and on improving your posture:

• Check your movement symmetry by looking at a pair of your old tennis shoes or Oxfords. Are the bottom of the shoes worn in a symmetrical pattern or is there a distinct difference between the left and right shoe?

• Watch a slowed-down home movie or videotape of your movements and try to observe the areas of your body that you hold back as you move.

In addition to imbalances in movement, the Colorado researchers cited the neurotransmitter serotonin as a possible contributor to chronic pain. Serotonin, which is believed to inhibit reflex action, may be depleted by spasms.

How can pain messages to the brain be interrupted?

We know that we can do it surgically by making tiny lesions with very fine instruments in the spinal cord or in the front of the brain.[11] This is a mechanical method that "cuts" the communication of even the most agonizing pain.

We can also do it chemically, but not as effectively, with pharmaceutical pain-killers. However, as scientists learn more and more about the brain's own neurotransmitters, more effective pain suppressants will be available. What has been learned thus far seems to explain why one of the most ancient pain-control methods works—counterirritation. Acupuncture, for example, more than 2,000 years old, involves the twirling of needles in tissues, to produce a deep, aching sensation. Cupping, in which a hot cup is placed on the skin, causes painful bruises and is almost as old as acupuncture. The Vietnamese rub a coin against the skin to treat pain. Athletic trainers today use ice to treat the injuries of athletes. The ice causes pain and so does electrical stimulation. Transcutaneous (through the skin) stimulators are increasingly popular electronic devices that are employed to treat all sorts of pain, from mild to severe. Pain inhibits pain, most likely by one pain perception interfering with the perception of another and affecting the release of neurotransmitters.

How much control do we have over our own neurotransmitters? We have potentially a great deal, but just as we don't use our full capacity to learn and perform, we don't use our full powers to modulate the chemical conversations that go on between our brains and our bodies.

STRESS AND HEART AND BRAIN CONVERSATIONS

The conversation between heart and brain during stress is probably most obvious. Remember how you felt when someone to whom you were very attracted sexually walked into the room, or when you sat in the dentist's chair awaiting the drilling? Your heart beat faster than usual. According to a husband-wife researcher team, John and Beatrice Lacey, at the Fels Research Institute, Yellow Springs, Ohio, not only is your heart rate sensitive to what your eyes see, but your eyes and brain respond as if controlled by the internal workings of your heart. There is a feedback. The Laceys maintain that the brain and heart/blood pressure form a feedback system with the brain continuously instructing the heart and the heart exhorting the brain. Under stressful conditions when it may be necessary to fight or flee, the heart accelerates, the blood pressure rises, and the body is prepared to react physically. On the other hand, when the brain is concentrating on an environmental or intellectual problem, the heart rate slows down.

In their experiments, the Laceys found that increases in heart rate and blood pressure interfere with attention to external environmental events, while decreases "tune in" the external world more sharply.[12]

BRAIN, HEART, AND PERSONALITY

So your heart affects your brain's ability to concentrate while your brain affects the ability of your heart to beat regularly.

In the 1970s, two San Francisco cardiologists, Ray Rosenman, M.D., and Meyer Friedman, M.D., described the personality type that was most prone to cardiovascular disease. People who were hard driving, competitive, and impatient were labeled Type A and said to be at greater risk than the more placid, labeled Type B.

In a study in the 1980s, the findings of Rosenman and Meyer held true, even in schoolboys. The blood pressure and heart rate of a group of youngsters were monitored as they played video games. The boys were then interviewed and their personality characteristics identified. Results of the study showed that the boys classified as Type As in interviews had a rise in blood pressure and heart rate greater than did those classified as Type Bs.

Dr. Karen A. Matthews, who directed the study, pointed out that normally, blood pressure and heart rate increase during any task performance. But those increases found in Type A boys were greater than in Type Bs, and the nature of their blood pressure changes indicated more involvement than the usual physiologic response.

The more placid boys' blood pressures went up an average of 10 millimeters of mercury, while the more competitive type had a 12-millimeter rise. Heartbeats for the competitive increased eight beats per minute, while the Type Bs had an increase of only three per minute.[13]

Research such as the investigation with the boys has led to the conclusion that part of your physical reaction to stress is genetic. Your brain perceives the environment and sends alerting chemical signals to your body with equipment inherited from your mother or father. Some people's nervous systems are more "sensitive" and react more strongly than others. However, you also learn through experience, just like Pavlov's dog, to react to certain situations with alarm. The big question is, How much control can you gain over your stress reactions, despite heredity and learning?

METHODS OF RELAXATION AND CONTROL

You can even gain control of those functions that western medical textbooks describe as involuntary, such as your digestion and heartbeat. Even your state of consciousness can be affected by how you voluntarily use your brain.

Eastern religious practitioners have known this all along. The yogis, for example, have emphasized the study and expansion of consciousness. They maintain that there is a positive realization of the body's capacities for sensory experience, for self-regulating of many body functions, and for avoiding the "aging" stresses in daily living. The yogis perform movements that consciously exercise the body and the mind together and have proven that humans can have amazing control over their own heartbeats and respirations.

Biofeedback

Western researchers today have applied learning and motivation to physiological functions formerly labeled involuntary and have constructed a scientific basis for what is now called *biofeedback*. The technique is based on the learning principle that a desired response is learned when received information (feedback) indicates that a specific thought or action has produced the desired response.

You use a form of biofeedback all the time. The simple act of maintaining your balance involves complex reflexes elicited by feedback from your eyes, your inner ear, your sense organs in muscles and joints. As you read this, tilt as far as you can off the side of the chair. Did you feel your neck and head trying to right your body? Information that you tilted slightly to one side elicited your reflexes to correct that tilt.

When these feedback mechanisms are disrupted, as in seasickness or zero gravity in space, nausea and other symptoms of motion sickness are often elicited. Yet people can be trained to control such symptoms by the use of biofeedback devices combined with relaxing imagery. The Air Force has found that such training can restore to flying status air crew who might otherwise be grounded because of air sickness.

Feedback and Imagery Test
Have someone place a hand, palm up, on your shoulder with the arm fully extended. Advise that person that you are going to try to bend his arm at the elbow joint, and that he should offer resistance. Notice the degree of difficulty required to bend his arm. Repeat the experiment, but this time ask him to envision his arm as a steel rod extending for miles beyond his hand. Now notice the difference in the exertion required to bend his arm. This shows the power of the mind to enhance performance.[14]

The primary difference between biofeedback and other self-regulation therapies is the use of electronic instrumentation that records and feeds back to you information about your body functions that you have never had before. The feedback may be in the form of a computerized video display or a simple light or tone that fluctuates along with the biological signal being monitored. With the use of such devices, and with the guidance of a biofeedback therapist, most people can easily learn to bring under voluntary control such phenomena as muscle tension and blood flow to the limbs. Among the types of activity that are monitored with biofeedback instruments are muscle or electromyographic (EMG) activity, changes in blood flow as measured through skin temperature, changes in EEG or brain wave activity, and changes in skin response (sweating), which track emotions or moods. Feedback is also used to monitor heart rate, respiration, gastrointestinal activity, and syphincters, which control movement of substances from one part of the GI (gastrointestinal) tract to another.

Biofeedback, which is used as an adjunct with other therapies such as medication and physiotherapy, is developing into a versatile and useful therapy. More than 10,000 papers have been published demonstrating the effectiveness of biofeedback for the management of more than 150 medical and psychological disorders.

Why does it work?

The most common explanation is that you become increasingly expert at discriminating internal body cues and adjusting your senses and muscles to them.

Neal Miller, Ph.D., professor emeritus and head of a laboratory of physiological psychology at Rockefeller University in New York, is the father of biofeedback. He maintains that through biofeedback it is now obvious that the mind cannot direct the activities of the body unless it has information about what is going on in the environment of the body, its tissues, and its cells. And we should have known that if the brain cannot operate without information from the body, and the body cannot operate without information from the brain, then both are not merely connected, they exist and function as a unit.

Dr. Miller says that most of us can control what we do with arms and legs, and with eye and face and other muscles, using the kind of body control called voluntary. But until recently, medical science believed and taught that nearly all our other body functions, such as blood flow, body temperature, brain waves, and even residual muscle tension itself, were under automatic regulation and beyond our control.[15]

Many other successful clinical applications of biofeedback, besides those mentioned in Dr. Miller's report, were presented at the 1985 Biofeedback Society of America meeting in New Orleans. Among them:

• Patients with Raynaud's Disease, who have painful constriction of the blood vessels in the fingers when exposed to cold, learned to raise the temperature in their hands through biofeedback at Wayne State University. These patients were thus able to reduce their constriction attacks by 93 percent over a three-year period.[16]

• Diabetics with leg and foot ulcers that would not heal were taught to raise the temperature of the affected limb and thus increase the blood supply. Two out of three patients at the Veterans Administration Hospital in Salt Lake City were able, with the aid of biofeedback, to induce healing of diabetic foot ulcers.[17]

• Six insulin-taking diabetics were taught to relax more effectively with biofeedback techniques at Georgetown University in Washington, D.C. As a result, they had decreased blood glucose levels, required less insulin, and had fewer incidences of great blood sugar fluctuations.[18]

• Patients with strabismus, crossed eyes or lazy eyes, were taught to control eye movement by biofeedback tone at the University of the Pacific in Forest Grove, Oregon. They typically had a failure of the neural control circuits that point and coordinate the eyes. When an eye deviates inward or outward, the brain is forced to deal with separate images from the two eyes. This can produce double vision, and the brain often corrects this problem by suppressing the output from one of the eyes, thus wasting its output. The patients learned to keep their eyes straight for two minutes in the dark or while viewing a blank white field.[19]

• Three patients with elevated inner-eye pressure—a condition that can cause blindness—were taught relaxation techniques through biofeedback at the University of Alabama in Birmingham. They achieved reduced intraocular pressure, probably because they reduced muscle tension around the eye. The researchers are continuing their investigation of the result.[20]

• A 57-year-old patient incapacitated with cerebral palsy was taught through biofeedback to control involuntary movements—jerking, twitching, tremor, and muscle spasms—through biofeedback. After a few months, he was able to dress himself, tie his own shoelaces, and walk eight to ten blocks. With fewer involuntary movements and less spasticity, he was able to fish from a boat and to climb stairs unaided, all of which he could not do before.[21]

• Twelve girls with curvature of the spine, which would normally have required a body brace, were taught —through the use of a halter that caused a bell to sound when they did not stand straight—to correct the curvature. Ten out of the twelve were able to avoid the brace.[22]

Biofeedback is also being used to train a person's brain to control its own brain waves. Two papers presented at the Biofeedback Society's 1985 meeting concerned training children with learning disabilities to overcome deficits through the use of brain-wave biofeedback.

Union, New Jersey, psychologist Michael Tansey, Ph.D., reported that he is training learning-disabled children to exercise the brain circuitry of their sensorimotor cortex (learning centers). Once aware of this brain-wave rhythm, they attempt to increase it. "Thus," Dr. Tansey said, "the brain may be viewed as a biological computer, the mind as a medium through which to access a cerebral (brain) exercise program with the electroencephalograph as a monitor, and the individual as a now-informed programmer."

Dr. Tansey claims that brain-wave training results in

improved hand-eye coordination, cessation of erratic eye movements, improved fine motor control in general and increased attentional flexibility, positive academic advancement through greater information-processing ability and memory capabilities, and increased IQ scores.[23]

Joel Lubar, Ph.D., of the University of Tennessee, and Judith Lubar, M.A., of the Southeastern Biofeedback Institute, reported at the same meeting that they recorded and analyzed the difference between the EEGs from the brains of 150 normal and learning-disabled children. Then through EEG biofeedback, they helped the learning-disabled youngsters to develop a more normal pattern. The youngsters attempted to increase the fast brainwave activity associated with concentration and attention, and at the same time to inhibit the slow brainwave activity and undesirable muscle activity, which might interfere with learning and concentration.[24]

Communicating directly with brain waves may also be possible, according to a report at the same meeting given by S. Thomas Elder, Ph.D., of the University of New Orleans, and his colleagues. They reported that their ultimate goal is to develop a method to allow patients suffering from the degenerative disease Amyotrophic Lateral Sclerosis (ALS), who are unable to move or speak but who can think, to communicate their needs. Through biofeedback, the researchers succeeded in teaching four volunteers to produce certain brain waves that caused a device to sound one tone for "yes" and another for "no" in response to questions.[25]

It is not surprising, therefore, that biofeedback has been successful with insomniacs and with migraine-headache sufferers. The former are taught to relax and allow sleep to arrive; the latter, how to raise the temperature in their hands to dilate blood vessels in spasm. In migraine, it is the blood vessels in the brain that dilate and cause pain. The body is designed to sacrifice blood flow to any other area in order to preserve blood flow to the brain. Therefore, the blood vessels in the hands constrict to shunt blood to the dilated blood vessels in the head during a migraine attack. As the hands are warmed, the blood vessels in them dilate and help, by a sort of reflex action, reduce the flow of blood to the brain.

Ease-a-Pain With Temperature Feedback
If you have a headache or pain elsewhere in your body, mark the intensity on the scale (shown on the opposite page) from 1 to 10. Hold an ordinary fever, meat, or household thermometer in your hand and place your elbow in a bowl or sink full of cold water. Wait two minutes and note the temperature on the thermometer. Then put your elbow in a bowl of warm water, about 100 to 103° F, and concentrate on the thermometer. Will your hand to get warmer and warmer. See if you can raise the mercury by at least 1 degree. Wait for five minutes and then write down the current intensity of your pain on the scale. Did it ease? With practice, you may greatly relieve your discomfort by this biofeedback hand-warming method.

The fact that you can "think" your hand warm is quite remarkable. No one is absolutely certain exactly how the brain and body work together to achieve this. However, it is believed that reward may be a large factor. You know that when you are trying to achieve something and you are cheered on or receive information that you are getting closer to your goal, you press onward. The information is a reward and helps you to keep trying until you succeed.

Do Your Own Biofeedback
Buying yourself a present when you've accomplished something that was difficult is a form of biofeedback. Looking at yourself naked in the mirror when your are on a diet is another form of biofeedback.

Ease-A-Pain Temperature Scale									
Day I		Day II		Day III		Day IV		Day V	
Before	After	Before	After	Before	After	Before	After	Before	After
10									
9									
8									
7									
6									
5									
4									
3									
2									
1									

If you have access to a blood pressure apparatus, the result of your trying consciously to lower your blood pressure may show you some remarkable results. It takes relaxation repetition and the will to do it along with the feedback from the numbers on the gauge.

Hypnosis

Hypnosis is an older method of mind over matter and stress reduction tool. The word *hypnosis* is derived from the name of the Greek god of sleep, Hypnos. While similar to sleep, hypnosis is actually a state of consciousness in which you are highly open to suggestion. In heterohypnosis, another person suggests the images, and in self-hypnosis, you do.

In order to experience hypnosis, there must be a sense of immediate involvement in one's mental imagery and detachment from the surrounding external environment. A variety of physiological and emotional states can be aroused or calmed. Hypnotic suggestions can be made in relation to the sensations of taste, touch, smell, and sight. Suggestions (known as posthypnotic) can also be made concerning expectations about forthcoming events.

The physiologic explanation of how and why hypnosis works to relieve stress and pain is yet to be made.[26] However, since the right side of the brain is concerned with diffuse, holistic, and intuitive thought and action, while the left brain is devoted more to analytic thinking, hypnosis is probably a right-brain phenomenon.

Indeed, when University of Washington researchers studied the brain waves of patients having wisdom teeth removed with hypnosis as the only anesthesia, the investigators found the dental patients' EEGs showed more activity on the right side of the brain.[27]

Drs. Ernest and Josephine Hilgard of Stanford University, two of the world's leading experts in the field, believe that human consciousness "flows" in more than one channel. That is, our awareness can take place at more than one level at the same time. Disassociation of the levels of our awareness occurs quite naturally. For instance, when we learn complex skills such as driving a car, we find initially that we have to pay full attention to each part of the task. As we become more expert, we can think of other things while driving and even talk to our companions. There is a wide variation in the ease with which people experience hypnosis but nearly everyone can. Those most difficult to hypnotize are the highly intellectual who constantly analyze and find it difficult to accept suggestions and the unintelligent who have little control over their conscious mind. The best subjects are those with average intelligence and a good imagination.[28]

Hypnotize Yourself
Exercise 1. Sit in a chair and look at a spot on the wall. Tell yourself that your eyelids are heavy, very heavy—so heavy you can't keep them open. Close your eyes slowly. Take five deep, slow breaths. Let your shoulders relax . . . your abdomen relax . . . your knees relax so they're apart. Tell yourself that your right arm is heavy, very heavy—so heavy that you can't hold it up. Keep concentrating on your right arm until you feel it is heavy. Then open your eyes and you will be able to just concentrate on your right arm and by association feel relaxed immediately. And you will be able to perform this autosuggestion relaxation anywhere, and at any time.
Exercise 2. Sit comfortably in a chair and do progressive relaxation. Tense the muscles of your toes for the count of 4, and relax for the count of 4. Tense your calf muscles for the count of 4 and relax for the count of 4. Continue tensing and relaxing your muscles all the way up to your forehead.
When you have finished, look straight ahead at the wall and try to keep your eyes open without blinking for the count of 50. (Don't you feel compelled to blink?)
Exercise 3. Think about your nose itching. Tell yourself

over and over that it itches and that you must scratch it. Keep thinking about it for two minutes—your nose tickles and you have to scratch it.

If you blinked or scratched your nose, you are in a state of suggestibility. Now repeat the relaxation exercise and then tell yourself in one phrase, something you wish to accomplish, such as:

"I am not going to let my boss upset me."

"I am going to win that tennis game tomorrow."

Repeat the phrase 15 times while keeping your body relaxed.

Eventually, you will be able to hypnotize yourself effectively without the relaxation exercises.

Smile and Benefit Your Brain

Hypnosis, of course, is a mental exercise, which can affect the physiology of brain and body. But can exercising the facial muscles to portray classic emotions also affect the physiology of the brain?

The theory that facial expressions affect brain function was first suggested more than 80 years ago by Israel Waynbaum, M.D., in a book published in Paris, *Physionomie Humaine: Son Mechanisme et Son Role Social*. Dr. Waynbaum maintained that all emotional reactions produce circulatory changes and affect blood flow to the brain. Smiling and laughing, the major expressions of happiness, increase blood flow and oxygen to the brain, while expressions of depression curb blood flow. The tears shed during hard laughter are nature's way of releasing pressure in the brain built up by the laughing.

If you find this hard to believe, look in the mirror. Put your fingers in your mouth and pull your lips into an exaggerated smile. Hold the expression for the count of 100. Look at the artery in your forehead. It should be pulsing noticeably because the muscles you are pulling act to impede the blood flow into the face and thus increase the pressure of blood in your brain.

Why do you furrow your brow when concentrating? By tightening the muscles in your forehead, you delay the flow of blood from the brain and allow the organ more nourishment for its harder work.

R. B. Zjonc, professor of psychology at the University of Michigan, points out that if brain temperature can influence moods by facilitating the release of particular neurotransmitters, and if facial musculature can modify brain temperature, then control of the appropriate facial muscles can induce more favorable moods. Yoga and various forms of meditation are based in part on such assumptions. Whether deliberate expressions have the same effectiveness as spontaneous ones is still to be proven.[29]

So there are many methods under investigation that can provide a greater understanding and control over stress. Biofeedback, hypnosis, and other relaxation techniques are widely used, effective aids. However, ultimately, the control over your own stress reactions is up to you. It may require changes in your lifestyle. Some of the alterations may be quite simple and others very difficult.

The following are techniques that have evolved over the years and have proved successful in alleviating stress. They are based on two approaches:

1. Controlling the sources of stress more effectively.
2. Creating a drain to relieve the tension.

WRITE DOWN YOUR MAJOR SOURCE(S) OF STRESS AT HOME:_____

_____

_____

WRITE DOWN YOUR MAJOR SOURCE(S) OF STRESS
AT WORK:_____

_____

_____

WRITE DOWN YOUR MAJOR SOURCE(S) OF STRESS
IN YOUR SOCIAL LIFE:_____

_____

_____

WRITE DOWN HOW YOU DEAL WITH THE
STRESSES THAT NOW AND THEN COME UP WITH
AT LEAST THREE IDEAS OF HOW YOU COULD
BETTER COPE WITH THE STRESSORS (you can dis-
cuss the ideas with friends or relatives):_____

_____

_____

Write a letter. You will not send it, but put down exactly
how you feel about the stressor. If the issue is doing the
dishes or if it is the way your mate or mother behaves at
a particular time, vent all your feelings. Put down all the
horrible things you wanted to say but never did.

Accept yourself. Tell yourself that everyone has mean
thoughts and that if you bury them, they don't go away.
They fester. Pamper yourself. If you get enough rest and
relaxation, you'll be better able to cope. It is better to have
a high opinion of yourself and be accused of being egotisti-
cal than a low opinion of yourself and find that others

accept your own evaluation. That's the road to depression and stress. If you love yourself, you'll be able to be more loving to others.[30]

Don't be a martyr. Learn to delegate responsibility. Training and motivating others to do tasks customarily performed by you can reduce your time burdens in the future. That's true at home and at work.

Think about communication. If you have never re-solved your conflicts from your childhood, perhaps it is time to reveal what you really feel. You don't have to put people on the defensive by saying, "You make me so made when . . ." or "I don't like it when you . . ." Instead, be open and say, "I wish you'd do it differently because . . ." or "Consider my feelings when this . . ." and let the person know in a nice way how his or her actions affect you.

Make a decision. It is better to make the wrong decision than to avoid making a decision at all. You have to decide now whether it will be A or B. Anybody can think of good reasons on both sides. But if you wait for 100 percent assurance, you'll wait forever. So make up your mind. Make the decision and carry it out. An error can be cor-rected, but indecision that causes stress can damage your brain and body.

Don't overdo details. Details can be completed, but sometimes a concern about small things leads to smallness in thinking. Some people become tense because they drown in their own details and then get pulled every which way worrying about them.

Don't insist on winning. Everybody loses sometime and you are no different from anyone else. Sometimes we benefit more by losing and trying again than by winning.

Don't wait for the sword to fall. If you are anxious about something and you can't talk yourself out of the anxiety, try to advance the event that is making you tense so that the anticipated occasion comes and goes in your mind. Note that you survived the event and think about that the next time you are worried about a future occurrence.

IDENTIFY YOUR GOALS

	TOMORROW	ONE YEAR	TEN YEARS
WORK			
PERSONAL			

Get sufficient sleep. Find your own personal sleep needs —whether it is four or ten hours a night. No one's brain works right when the body is fatigued.

Relax as soon as you are fatigued. If you wait until you are completely exhausted, you will be tense and it will be more difficult for you to recuperate.

Remember that sex may be good for your brain. Studies have shown that sexual stimulation releases endorphins in the brain and not only eases tension, but relieves the pain of arthritis and other ailments. Animal studies have shown that stimulation of the genitals increases brain metabolism.[31] So, if you need a good excuse to have sex, there it is. Sex will help you think better.

Stop making excuses. As we have described repeatedly, your brain has amazing powers that remain vital if you continue to exercise them well into old age. Don't concentrate on the "if onlys" and the "I would have, buts." You can't change your parents, the place of your birth, your brothers and sisters, or your talents—but you can make the most of what you've got. Take action!

11

Beyond Imagination

With your eyes shut, picture a bottle.
Turn the bottle upside down.
Make it smaller.
Make it larger.
Change the shape of it.
Change the color of it.
Bring it up as close to you as you can.

Open your eyes! You have now demonstrated the marvelous things only your brain can do.

You really do have the ability to perform better, to use more of your potential, and to be a happier, more effective person.

A computer is a wondrous machine. It can remember millions of bits of information and if you press the right button, it will recall a specific bit of data. But a computer cannot really think. It cannot recognize the face of someone at a 25th class reunion who's put on weight, lost his hair, and only vaguely resembles his former self. Even though your brain retains the old image, it can still deal with the changes and recognize your old classmate.

Raymond Truex and Malcolm Carpenter pointed out in their text *Human Neuroanatomy:*

"Electronic brains" are impressive in appearance and function; yet they do not approach in versatility or scope the fantastic potentialities of the human brain. The human brain is unique in that it can provide its own programming; in fact, it is programmed throughout life by our daily experience. It seems likely that "electronic brains" will in the future perform many more of the functions now performed by human brains, but this change must be regarded as a redistribution of labor, not a replacement. The "electronic brain" is after all only one of the many expressions of the ingenuity of the human brain.[1]

There is one thing that both the computer and the brain require—an input to produce an output. Too often, in our culture, we stop inputting a lot of new data into our brains after a certain age. We don't respect the capacity of the older brain.

Ella Tuttle Mattheson, a 102-year-old columnist for the *Clinton, Local* newspaper in Clinton, Michigan, maintains: "My memory is as sharp today as it ever was. It's just that I have to tax it a little more. But then, I've got a lot more to remember than anyone else."[2]

Dorothy Fuldheim, the feisty Midwest broadcaster in her ninth decade, put it succinctly: "It gets my goat when people say it's remarkable how bright I am at my age. I was bright forty years ago. And the more I use my brain, the sharper it gets."[3]

We couldn't agree more.

The future of human brain research is nearly beyond imagination.

As the neurosciences progress, it will be possible to further protect and enhance brain function. Successful transplantation of brain tissue will be accomplished and disabilities overcome. There will soon be drugs to strengthen failing memories and to increase concentration. The riddles of the chemical aberrations that cause schizophrenia and autism will be solved.

Techniques in the field of cognitive rehabilitation will be further perfected, and lost function due to strokes and accidents will be restored to a greater degree.

As we have pointed out throughout this book, great progress has already been made in understanding the brain and its effect on the body functions and the body's effect on the brain. It has been proven that the continued development of your brain is not significantly limited by your age. The potential is there. You can learn to handle environmental stress so that it does not damage your brain and body. You can gain greater control over the stimulation your brain receives and the signals it puts out.

The advance of technology only now permits probing inside the living brain to interpret function. Neuroscientists can see metabolism and flow as related to function, but they cannot yet determine creativity nor evaluate finite potential. They cannot measure motivation.

What you do with your brain—how you challenge it and exercise it to keep it in top form and to achieve its full potential—well, that's all in *your* head!

Notes

CHAPTER 1: THE PLASTIC BRAIN AND HOW IT GROWS

1. "Senility Reconsidered: Treatment Possibilities for Mental Impairment in the Elderly," Task Force sponsored by the National Institute on Aging, Bethesda, Md., *Journal of the American Medical Society* (July 18, 1980): 259–260.

2. R. Duara, M.D., et al., "Cerebral Glucose Utilization as Measured with Positron Emission Tomography in 21 Resting Healthy Men Between the Ages of 21 and 83 Years," *Brain*, 106 (1983): 761–775.

3. K. Warner Schaie, ed., *Longitudinal Studies of Adult Psychological Development* (New York: Guilford Press, 1983).

4. Marian Cleeves Diamond, Ph.D., and James R. Connor, Department of Physiology, University of California at Berkeley, paper presented at the Tenth Annual Meeting of the Society for Neuroscience, Cincinnati, Ohio, Nov. 9–10, 1980.

5. Ruth Winter, "Biomarkers: Beating Body Burnout," *American Health*, May 1984, 70–80.

6. Mark R. Rosenzweig, Ph.D., and Edward Bennett, Ph.D., University of California, Lawrence Berkeley Laboratory, June 24, 1980; "The Physiological Imprint of Learning," U.S. Department of Health Research Grant Report, National Institutes of Health, May 1966.

7. John R. Sladek, Jr., Ph.D., and Carol Phelps, Ph.D., paper presented at the International Catecholamine Symposium, Gotenborg, Sweden, June 12, 1983.

8. Ranjan Duara, M.D., interview with authors, National Institutes of Health, Bethesda, Md., April 13, 1984.

9. National Institute of Medicine Report, Washington, D.C., March 31, 1981.

10. Winter, op. cit.

11. Ibid.

12. Bernice Grafstein, Cornell University Medical College, speech presented to the Society for Neuroscience Science Writers Seminar, New York, Nov. 9, 1976.

13. Carmelita G. Frondoza, Reinhard Grzanna, and Richard Humphrey, "Effects of 6-Hydroxydopamine and Reserpine on the Growth of LPC-1 Plasmacytoma," paper presented at the Annual Meeting of the Society for Neuroscience, Boston, Mass., Nov. 7, 1983.

14. T. G. Saith, Jr., M.D., Laboratory of Neurophysiology, paper presented at the Society for Neuroscience meeting, Atlanta, Ga., Nov. 6, 1979.

15. Sladek and Phelps, op. cit.

16. Diamond, op. cit.

17. Schaie, op. cit.

18. Rosenzweig and Bennett, op. cit.

19. Elizabeth A. McCusker, M.B., B.S., et al., "Recovery from Locked-In Syndrome," *Archives of Neurology,* 39(3) (March 1982): 145–147.

20. Joan O'Connor, "Research Using Head-Injured Vietnam Veterans Shows Effects of Brain Lesions on Mental Performance," *Psychiatric News,* May 17, 1985.

21. Ruth Levine, "Reorganizing the Brain," *Touchstone,* 18(3), University of Wisconsin–Madison Research Program (December 1984).

22. Malcolm L. Meltzer, Ph.D., "Poor Memory: A Case Report," *Journal of Clinical Psychology* (January 1983): 1–10.

23. Malcolm L. Meltzer, Ph.D., communication with authors, Washington, D.C., July 1984.

24. O'Connor, op. cit.

25. Irwin Pollock, M.D., Herbert Kohn, Ph.D., and

Michael Miller, Ph.D., "Rehabilitation of Cognitive Function in Brain-Damaged Persons," *Journal of the Medical Society of New Jersey*, 81(4) (April 1984): 311–315.
26. Irwin Pollock, M.D., interview with author, New Brunswick, N.J., May 2, 1984.
27. Irene Parese, Ph.D., interview with authors, Kessler Institute, East Orange, N.J., May 16, 1984.

CHAPTER 2: HOW TO BE SENSATIONAL—PERFECTING YOUR PERCEPTIONS

1. John Kubie et al., Downstate Medical Center, Brooklyn, N.Y., "Manipulations of the Geometry of Environmental Enclosures Control the Spatial Firing Patterns of Hippocampal Neurons," paper presented at the Society for Neuroscience meeting, Boston, Mass., Nov. 9, 1983.
2. Stephen K. Itaya, Ph.D., "Retinal Inputs to Limbic, Auditory and Motor Areas in the Rat," paper presented at the Society for Neuroscience meeting, Cincinnati, Ohio, Nov. 9, 1980.
3. Mark Rosenzweig, Ph.D., David Krech, Ph.D., and Marian Diamond, Ph.D., "The Physiologic Imprint of Learning Investigators," paper prepared by Gay Luce after interviews in December 1965 and May 1966, National Institutes of Health publication.
4. David Hubel and Torsten Wiesel, "Receptive Fields, Binocular Interaction and Functional Architecture in a Cat's Visual Cortex," *Journal of Physiology* (London) 160 (1962): 106–154; and "Shape and Arrangement of Columns in a Cat's Striate Cortex," *Journal of Physiology* (London) 165 (1962–63): 559–568.
5. Dr. Donald Kline, associate professor of psychology, University of Notre Dame, Notre Dame, Ind., report of National Institute of Health's Research Career Development, March 16, 1984.
6. Jane Brody, "Surprising Health Impact Discovered for Light," *New York Times* (Nov. 13, 1984): C1.
7. "How Today's Noise Hurts Body and Mind," *Medical World News* (June 13, 1969): 42–43.

8. M. D. Safranek, "Effect of Auditory Rhythm on Muscle Reactivity," *Physical Therapy* (February 1982): 161–188.

9. *Medical World News*, op. cit.

10. Ruth Winter, *The Smell Book* (New York: J. P. Lippincott, 1978), 201–202.

11. R. C. Trux et al., *Human Neuroanatomy* (Baltimore, Md.: Williams and Wilkins, 1964), 436.

12. Susan Schiffman, Ph.D., "Taste and Smell in Disease (Part One)," *New England Journal of Medicine*, 308(21) (May 26, 1983): 1275–1279; and "Taste and Smell in Disease (Part Two)," *New England Journal of Medicine*, 308(22) (June 2, 1983): 1337–1343.

13. James Weifeenbach, Ph.D., ed., "Taste and Development: The Genesis of Sweet Preference," National Institute of Dental Research, U.S. Department of Health, Bethesda, Md., 1977, No. (ADM) 75–236.

14. Ashley Montagu, *Touching: The Human Significance of the Skin* (New York: Perennial, 1972).

15. Michael Curley, Ph.D., and Robert Hawkins, Ph.D., "Cognitive Performance During a Heat Acclimatization Regimen," *Aviation Space Environmental Medicine* (August 1983): 709–713.

CHAPTER 3: IMPROVING THE COORDINATION OF BRAIN, MUSCLE, AND NERVE

1. E. V. Evarts, "Brain Mechanisms in Voluntary Movements," *Scientific American*, September 1979, 164–179.

2. Carol Phelps and John R. Sladek, Department of Anatomy, University of Rochester, "Regeneration of Central Catecholamine Fibers in Aged Rats," paper presented at the Society for Neuroscience meeting, Boston, Mass., Nov. 10, 1983.

3. Walter Kroll, University of Massachusetts, interview with author, October 1984, and various papers.

4. K. V. Anderson et al., "Neuromuscular Control Mechanism in Oromotor Behavior," paper presented at the Society for Neuroscience meeting, Anaheim, Calif., Oct. 11, 1984.

5. R. J. Nelson et al., "Variations in the Proportional Representations of the Hand in Somatosensory Cortex of Primates," paper presented at the Society for Neuroscience meeting, Boston, Mass., Nov. 13, 1980.

6. W. M. Jenkins, M. M. Merzenich, and M. T. Ochs, Coleman Memorial Labs, Department of Otolaryngology and Physiology, University of California at San Francisco, paper presented at the Society for Nueroscience meeting, Anaheim, Calif., Oct. 13, 1984.

7. Kroll, op. cit.

8. Special Report on Aging, February 1980, and Seminar for Science Writers, Bethesda, Md., January 1981.

9. "The Cerebellum: Loss of Cellular Function in the Aging Brain," *The Salk Institute News Letter*, 27 (Winter 1981): 1–4.

10. Mark Williams, M.D., University of Rochester, interview with author, April 1984.

11. Special Report on Aging, U.S. Department of Health, NIH Publication No. 80-2135, August 1980.

CHAPTER 4: AEROBICS FOR THE BRAIN

1. Charles Ransford, "A Role for Amines in the Antidepressant Effect of Exercise: A Review," *Medicine and Science in Sports and Exercise*, 12(1) (1982): 1–10.

2. B. S. Brown et al., "Chronic Response of Rat Brain Norepinephrine and Serotonin to Endurance Training," *Journal of Applied Physiology*, 46 (1979): 19–23.

3. Robert E. Dustman et al., "Aerobic Exercise Training and Improved Neuropsychological Function of Older Individuals," *Neurobiology of Aging*, Fayetteville, N.Y. (Spring 1984): 35–42.

4. Caryle H. Folkins and Wesley Sime, "Physical Fitness Training and Mental Health," *American Psychologist* (April 1981): 373–389.

5. R. J. Young, Ph.D., "The Effect of Regular Exercise on Cognitive Functioning and Personality," *British Journal of Sports Medicine*, 13 (1979): 110–117.

6. Patricia Del Rey, "Effects of Contextual Interference of

the Memory of Older Females in Differing Levels of Physical Activity," *Perceptual and Motor Skills,* 6(2) (April 10, 1983): 171–180.

7. M. Elsayed et al., "Intellectual Difference of Adult Men Related to Age and Physical Fitness Before and After an Exercise Program," *Journal of Gerontology* (May 1980): 383–387.

8. Dr. Daniel B. Carr et al., "Physical Conditioning Facilitates the Exercise-Induced Secretion of Beta-Endorphin and Beta-Lipotropin in Women," *The New England Journal of Medicine,* 305(10) (Sept. 3, 1981): 560–563.

9. David Sinyor et al., "Aerobic Fitness Level and Reactivity to Psychosocial Stress, Physiological, Biochemical and Subjective Measure," *Psychosomatic Medicine,* 45 (June 1983): 205–214.

10. "Jogging for Mental Health: Believers and Skeptics Collide," *Psychiatric News* (Sept. 16, 1983): 38–39.

11. Sharla Lichtman and Ernest Poser, "The Effects of Exercise on Mood and Cognitive Functioning," *Journal of Psychosomatic Research* 27(11) (1983): 43–52.

12. Richard Powell, "Technique for Differentiating Cortical Hemispheric Activity Following Exercise," *Perceptual and Motor Skills* 54 (June 1982): 923–932.

13. Erik Peper, Ph.D., Center for Interdisciplinary Science, San Francisco State University, "The Treatment of Asthma: Combining Biofeedback Family Therapy and Self-Regulation," paper presented at the Society for Biofeedback of America meeting, New Orleans, La., April 14, 1985.

14. Ruth Winter, "Fitness Benefits," *Harper's Bazaar,* August 1982, 148–150.

CHAPTER 5: MUSIC FOR THE MIND

1. Daniel Margoliash, M.D., "An Auditory Representation of the Bird's Own Song," paper presented at the Society for Neuroscience meeting, Anaheim, Calif., Oct. 11, 1984.

2. "New Insights Explain Movement Control by the Brain," *News and Features,* The National Institutes of Health, April 1984.

3. Ruth Winter, "Music: The New Active Sport," *Self,* May 1984, 175.

4. Manfred Schroeder, Ph.D., researcher, AT&T Bell Laboratories, "Monaural Phase Effects in Masking with Multicomponent Signals," Symposium on Hearing-Physiological Bases and Psychophysics, Bad Nauheim, West Germany, April 5–9, 1983.

5. Winter, op. cit.

6. M. G. Safranek, "Effect of Auditory Rhythms on Muscle Activity," *Physical Therapy,* 62(2) (February 1982): 161–168.

7. Winter, op. cit.

8. Ibid.

9. "Scheming of Human Brain Helps Overcome Language Impairment," Stanford University Medical Center release, Feb. 8, 1984.

10. Winter, op. cit.

11. R. J. Trotter, "The Sight of Music Read in the Face," *Psychology Today,* March 18, 1985.

12. Winter, op. cit.

13. Ibid.

14. Ibid.

CHAPTER 6: MEMORIES ARE MADE OF . . .

1. Marian Cleeves Diamond, "The Aging Rat Forebrain: Male-Female Left-Right: Environment and Lipofuscin," in *Aging of the Brain.,* ed. D. Samuel et al. (New York: Raven Press, 1983), 93–98.

2. Max V. Mathews, David E. Meyer, and Saul Sternberg, "Exploring the Speed of Mental Processes," Bell Laboratories *Record,* Murray Hill, N.J., March 1975, 150–156.

3. W. Penfield and B. Milner, "Memory Deficit Produced by Bilateral Lesions of the Hippocampal Zone," *American*

Medical Association Archives of Neurology and Psychiatry, 7 (1958): 475.

4. S. J. Y. Nizumori et al., "Age-Related Increased Susceptibility to Anisomycin-Induced Amnesia in Mice: Effects of Prolonged Treatment With Dietary Choline," paper presented at the Society for Neuroscience meeting, Boston, Mass., Nov. 7, 1983.

5. K. Anders Ericsoon et al., "Aquisition of a Memory Skill," *Science*, 208 (June 6, 1980): 1181–1182.

CHAPTER 7: INCREASE YOUR ABILITY TO LEARN

1. K. Warner Schaie, ed., *Longitudinal Studies of Adult Psychological Development* (Guilford, N.Y., 1983).

2. Ruth Winter, "Are You as Smart as You Once Were?" *Register and Tribune Syndicate*, Des Moines, Iowa, Feb. 7, 1982.

3. Raymond B. Cattell, *Abilities: Their Structure, Growth and Action* (Boston: Houghton Mifflin, 1971).

4. Winter, op. cit.

5. Gregory Clark, "Cell Biological Analysis of Associative and Non-Associative Learning," paper presented at the Annual Meeting of the American Association for the Advancement of Science, New York, May 26, 1984.

6. University of Illinois at Urbana *News Feature*, Dec. 18, 1980.

7. Eric Kandel and James Schwartz, "Molecular Biology of Learning: Modulation of Neurotransmitter Release," *Science*, 218 (Oct. 29, 1982): 433–442.

8. Special Report on Aging, U.S. Department of Health, NIH Pub. No. 80-1907, February 1980.

9. "A Window to the Brain: Where Linguistics and the Brain Sciences Meet, Insights Flow in Both Directions," *Mosaic*, 7 (March–April 1976): 14–25.

CHAPTER 8: MINING YOUR CREATIVITY

1. "Visionaries and Madmen: Are Creativity and Schizophrenia Linked?" University of California *Clip Sheet*, Berkeley, Calif., 53(10) (Oct. 1, 1977).

2. Ibid.

3. Frederic F. Flach, M.D., "A Reappraisal of the Creative Process," *Psychiatric Annals*, 8(3) (March 1978): 11–22.

4. Frederic F. Flach, M.D., interview with author, New York, April 27, 1975.

5. Jan Ehrenwald, M.D., *The Anatomy of Genius: Split Brains and Global Minds* (New York: Human Science Press, 1984).

6. Beth Ann Krier, "Engineers Work on Developing the 'Fun Sides' of Their Brains," *Los Angeles Times*, March 16, 1984.

7. Jerre Levy and M. Reid, "Variations in Writing Posture and Cerebral Organization," *Science*, 194 (1976): 337–339.

8. Frederic F. Flach, interview with author.

9. Morris Stein, Ph.D., "Methods to Stimulate Creative Thinking," *Psychiatric Annals*, 8(3) (March 1978): 65.

10. Bernice Neugarten and D. Gutman, *Age-Sex Roles and Personality in Middle Age: A Thematic Apperception Study in Middle Age and Aging* (Chicago: Chicago University Press, 1975).

CHAPTER 9: FOOD FOR THOUGHT

1. Sheryl Grady et al., "Neuropsychological Function and Regional Cerebral Glucose Utilization in Healthy Aging and Dementia," paper presented at the Society for Neuroscience meeting, Boston, Mass., Nov. 10, 1983.

2. A. Pulsinelli et al., "Diabetes Mellitus," *Journal of the American Medical Association*, 74 (1983): 540–544.

3. *Science News*, Aug. 20, 1983.

4. *Good Housekeeping*, February 1984, 222.

5. Ibid.

6. G. Frank Lawliss, Ph.D., et al., "Impacts of Food and Chemicals on Behavior," paper presented at the American Psychological Association meeting, Toronto, Canada, Aug. 27, 1984.

7. W. C. Abraham, Ph.D., et al., "Chronic Ethanol Effects on Sympathetic Function and Distribution in the Rat Hippocampus," paper presented at the Tenth Annual

Meeting of the Society for Neuroscience, Cincinnati, Ohio, Nov. 10, 1980.

8. Bernice Porjesz and Henri Begleiter, "Evoked Brain Potential Differentiation Between Geriatric Subjects and Chronic Alcoholics With Brain Dysfunction," *Annals Neurology*, 32 (1982): 117–124.

9. Allen Neims and Reidvon Borsetl, "Caffeine: Metabolism and Biochemical Action," in *Nutrition and the Brain* (Vol. 6), eds. R. J. Wurtman and J. J. Wurtman (New York: Raven Press, 1983), 1–30.

10. Peter Morgane, Worcester Foundation for Experimental Biology, Shrewsbury, Mass., interview with author, March 27, 1977.

11. A. J. Gelenberg et al., "Tyrosine for the Treatment of Depression," *American Journal of Psychiatric Research*, 17(2) (1982–83): 175–180.

12. *Good Housekeeping*, February 1984, 222.

13. Alan F. Sved, "Precursor Control of the Functions of Monoaminergic Neurons," in *Nutrition and the Brain* (Vol. 6), eds. R. J. Wurtman and J. J. Wurtman (New York: Raven Press, 1983): 223–275.

14. R. T. Bartus et al., "Age-Related Changes in Passive Avoidance Retention: Modulations With Dietary Choline," *Science*, 209 (July 11, 1980): 301–303.

15. Arthur Winter, M.D., "New Treatment for Multiple Sclerosis," *Neurological and Orthopedic Journal of Medicine and Surgery*, 5 (April 1, 1984): 39–43.

16. Ruth Winter, *Register and Tribune* column, Des Moines, Iowa, Jan. 2, 1983.

17. *Psychiatric News*, July 1, 1983.

18. E. Pollitt and R. L. Leibel, "Iron Deficiency and Behavior," *Journal of Pediatrics*, 88(3) (1976): 372–381.

19. Ibid.

20. "Zinc Deficiency Retards Brain Development in Rat Studies," U.S. Department of Agriculture Report, Washington D.C., Nov. 10, 1983.

21. Peter Morgane, "Historical and Modern Concepts of Hypothalamic Organization and Function," in *Handbook of the Hypothalamus*, eds. P. J. Morgane and J. Pankseep (New York: Marcel Dekker, 1980): 1–64.

22. *Medical World News,* New York, Oct. 22, 1971.

23. Benjamin Feingold, M.D., *Why Is Your Child Hyperactive?* (New York: Random House, 1975).

24. Ruth Winter, *Consumers Dictionary of Food Additives* rev. ed. (New York: Crown Publishers, 1984): 1–17.

25. John Salvaggio, M.D., ed., et al. "Primer on Allergic and Immunological Diseases," American Academy of Allergic and Immunological Diseases, Chicago, *Journal of the American Medical Association* (Nov. 26, 1982): 2579–2637.

26. John W. Crayton, M.D., associate professor of psychiatry, University of Chicago, "Adverse Reactions to Foods: Relevance to Psychiatric Disorders," report, University of Chicago, Illinois 60637, May 1985.

27. Ruth Winter, "Food Diary to Help You Uncover a Food Allergy," in *The People's Handbook of Allergies and Allergens* (Chicago: Contemporary Books, 1984): 128–129.

28. David Margulies, Beatriz Moisset, Michael Lewis, Hauo Shibiga, and Candace Pert, "Beta Endorphin Is Associated With Overeating in Genetically Obese Mice and Rats," *Science,* 202 (Dec. 1, 1978): 89–99.

CHAPTER 10: PROTECTING YOUR BRAIN FROM STRESS

1. Mary F. Asterita, Ph.D., Indiana University School of Medicine, paper presented at the Biofeedback Society of America meeting, New Orleans, April 13, 1985.

2. K. J. Helsing et al., "Causes of Death in Widowed Population," *American Journal of Epidemiology,* 116(3) (September 1982): 524–532.

3. Ester Fride, Martha Weinstock, and M. Gavish, paper presented at the Society for Neuroscience meeting, Boston, Mass., Nov. 8, 1983.

4. *Special Report on Aging,* U.S. Department of Health, NIH. No. 80-2135, August 1980.

5. Bruce McEwen, Ph.D., *Rockefeller University Research Profile,* Spring 1984.

6. Troell S. Jensen, M.D., et al., "Cerebral Atrophy in Young Torture Victims," *New England Journal of Medicine,* 307(21) (Nov. 18, 1982): 1341.

7. Richard S. Lazarus, "A Cognitively Oriented Psychologist Looks at Biofeedback," *American Psychologist,* 30 (1975): 553–561.

8. Donald G. Payan, M.D., University of California, San Francisco, "Substance P," paper presented at the American Association for the Advancement of Science meeting, Los Angeles, Calif., May 30, 1985.

9. *Psychiatric News,* April 5, 1985.

10. Edgar Wilson, M.D., and Carol Schneider, Ph.D., University of Colorado, "Static and Dynamic Biofeedback in the Treatment of Chronic Muscle Pain," paper presented at the Biofeedback Society of America meeting, New Orleans, La., April 16, 1985.

11. Arthur Winter, M.D., *Surgical Control of Behavior* (Springfield, Ill.: Chas. Thomas, 1971).

12. Sam Rosenfeld, "Conversations Between Heart and Brain," U.S. Department of Health, No. 017-024000764-1, November 1977.

13. Cardiovascular Research Report, American Heart Association, Summer 1982.

14. Erik Peper, Ph.D., San Francisco State University, Calif., various papers and reprints presented at the Biofeedback Society of America meeting, New Orleans, La., April 14–16, 1985.

15. Neal Miller, Ph.D., Rockefeller University, New York, "Some Professional and Scientific Problems and Opportunities for Biofeedback," paper presented at the Biofeedback Society of America meeting, New Orleans, La., April 14, 1985.

16. Albert Freedman, Ph.D., et al., Lafayette Clinic and Wayne State University, "Beta-Adrenergic Vasodilating Mechanism in Temperature Biofeedback," paper presented at the Biofeedback Society of America meeting, New Orleans, La., April 14, 1985.

17. Aharon D. Shulimson, M.S., et al., "Diabetic Ulcers: The Effect of Thermal Biofeedback on Healing," paper presented at the Biofeedback Society of America meeting, New Orleans, La., April 13, 1985.

18. Lilian Rosenbaum, Ph.D., clinical associate professor and

director, Biofeedback Programs, Georgetown University Hospital, Washington, D.C., "A Team Approach to Diabetes: Biofeedback-Family Therapist, Nurse, Educator, Dietician and Diabetologist," paper presented at the Biofeedback Society of America meeting, New Orleans, La., April 14, 1985.

19. Robert Yolton, Ph.D., College of Optometry, Pacific University, Forest Grove, Oregon, "Biofeedback Treatment of Strabismus," presented at the Biofeedback Society of America meeting, New Orleans, La., April 16, 1985.

20. James Raczynski, Ph.D., director, Psychophysiological Services, University of Alabama, Birmingham, "Biofeedback Treatment of Elevated Intraocular Pressure," paper presented at the Biofeedback Society of America meeting, New Orleans, La., April 16, 1985.

21. Marcella Fischer-Williams, M.D., et al., "Cerebral Palsy Treated With EMG Biofeedback Following Neurosurgery," paper presented at the Biofeedback Society of America meeting, New Orleans, La., April 13, 1985.

22. Miller, op. cit.

23. Michael Tansey, Ph.D., Union, N.J., "Sensorimotor Rhythm Biofeedback Training: Its Clinical Application for Learning Disabilities," paper presented at the Biofeedback Society of America meeting, New Orleans, La., April 16, 1985.

24. Joel Lubar, Ph.D., and Judith Lubar, M.A., paper presented at the Biofeedback Society of America meeting, New Orleans, La., April 16, 1985.

25. S. Thomas Elder, Ph.D., University of New Orleans, paper presented at the Biofeedback Society of America meeting, New Orleans, La., April 14, 1985.

26. A.C.N. Chen and S. F. Dworkin, University of Washington, paper presented at the American Pain Society meeting, San Diego, Calif., Sept. 9, 1979.

27. Ibid.

28. "Doctors Shun Hypnotism's Power to Ease Pain, Say Stanford Experts," *Stanford University News Service* feature, Dec. 19, 1983.

29. R. B. Zjonc, "Emotions and Facial Efference: A Theory Reclaimed," *Science,* April 5, 1985.

30. Vega Militariu, psychologist, Culinary Institute of America, interview with author, Hyde Park, N.Y., Dec. 19, 1982.

31. T. O. Allen, N. T. Adler, J. H. Greenberg, and M. Reivich, "Vaginocervical Stimulation Selectively Increases Metabolic Activity in the Rat Brain," *Science,* 211 (March 6, 1981).

CHAPTER 11: BEYOND IMAGINATION

1. Raymond Truex and Malcolm Carpenter, *Human Neuroanatomy* (Baltimore, Md.: William and Wilkins Co., 1964), 504.

2. "The Writing Life: It Takes Guts to Grow Old," *Writers Digest,* October 1983, 20–21.

3. *New Woman,* October 1984.

Index